GATEWAY
to GOD'S
BLESSING

GATEWAY to GOD'S BLESSING

DEREK PRINCE

WHITAKER
HOUSE

GATEWAY TO GOD'S BLESSING

Derek Prince Ministries
P.O. Box 19501
Charlotte, North Carolina 28219
www.derekprince.org

ISBN-13: 978-1-60374-052-4
ISBN-10: 1-60374-052-X
Printed in the United States of America
© 2008 by Derek Prince Ministries, International

Whitaker House
1030 Hunt Valley Circle
New Kensington, PA 15068
www.whitakerhouse.com

Library of Congress Cataloging-in-Publication Data

Prince, Derek.
Gateway to God's blessing / by Derek Prince.
p.   cm.
Summary: "Explains how the biblical concept of the fear of the Lord is the source of wisdom and humility"—Provided by publisher.
ISBN 978-1-60374-052-4 (trade pbk. : alk. paper) 1. God (Christianity)—Worship and love. 2. Fear of God—Christianity.
I. Title.
BV4817.P75 2008
231'.7—dc22   2008009607

1 2 3 4 5 6 7 8 9 10 **WH** 14 13 12 11 10 09 08

CONTENTS

1. God's Strength and God's Wisdom 7

2. The Measure of True Strength 15

3. Exchanging Strength 21

4. The Grain of Wheat 29

5. Those Who Learned to Yield 37

6. Up Is Down 49

7. God's Purpose for Man 63

8. Down Is Up 77

9. Do We Fear the Lord? 107

10. The Conditions We Must Meet............ 125

11. Benefits and Blessings...................... 129

12. The Key to a Perfect Heart 151

13. Our Response.................................. 165

About the Author 173

CHAPTER ONE

God's Strength and God's Wisdom

So much of the Bible—and of the Christian faith—is directly contrary to the wisdom and the ways of this world. The world thinks a certain way; it has certain standards and operates on certain principles.

But what God reveals in His Word is usually directly contrary to this. One of the priceless blessings of the Bible is that it enables us to approach and navigate this life from God's point of view so that we can avoid being ensnared by worldly lusts and sinful ways.

The prophet Isaiah tells us in vivid language how far God's ways and God's thoughts are from those of man. Speaking on behalf of God, he said,

> *"My thoughts are not your thoughts, nor are your ways My ways," says the LORD. "For as the heavens are higher than the earth, so are My ways higher than your ways, and My thoughts than your thoughts."* (Isaiah 55:8–9)

There is a tremendous gap that man cannot bridge between the level of God's ways and the level of man's ways. Man's ways are on an earthly plane; God's ways are on a heavenly plane.

There is good news, however: God has provided a means by which His ways and His thoughts can be brought down to our earthly level and actually be imparted to us. This happens through His Word.

And so in the next two verses of Isaiah 55, God continues to speak through the prophet:

> *For as the rain comes down, and the snow from heaven, and do not return there, but water the earth, and make it bring forth and bud, that it may give seed to the sower and bread to the eater, so shall My word be that goes*

*forth from My mouth; it shall not return
to Me void, but it shall accomplish what
I please, and it shall prosper in the thing
for which I sent it.* (Isaiah 55:10–11)

God is saying that just as the rain and
the snow come down from heaven to make the
earth fruitful, so too His Word will go out and
accomplish His purposes.

This idea applies to the difference between
the strength and wisdom of God and the
strength and wisdom of man. God's standards
are totally different from ours, but through
His Word, we can come to see these things
from His point of view.

In the New Testament, Paul also set forth
the difference between God's standards of
strength and wisdom and the standards of
this world:

*For Jews request a sign, and Greeks
seek after wisdom; but we preach Christ
crucified, to the Jews a stumbling block
and to the Greeks foolishness, but to
those who are called, both Jews and
Greeks, Christ the power of God and
the wisdom of God. Because the foolishness of God is wiser than men, and*

the weakness of God is stronger than men.   (1 Corinthians 1:22–25)

In the *New International Version* verse 25 reads, *"For the foolishness of God is wiser than man's wisdom, and the weakness of God is stronger than man's strength."* What is foolishness and weakness in the eyes of the world is wisdom and strength from God's perspective.

It is important to notice that Paul uses just two words to define God's foolishness and God's weakness: *"Christ crucified"* (verse 23). It is the crucifixion of Jesus that is God's "foolishness" and God's "weakness," and yet this "foolishness" is wiser and stronger than anything men can set against it. The cross—the ultimate emblem of shame, weakness, and defeat—is the key to glory, power, wisdom, and victory. That is the remarkable difference between God's ways and man's ways.

The crucifixion was not an unplanned disaster.

We need to remember that God planned the crucifixion. It was not an unexpected disaster for which God had to make provision. Rather, it was the fulfillment of a divine plan—the expression of God's wisdom and God's strength.

Speaking about the death of Jesus to the Jewish people on the day of Pentecost, Peter said about Jesus:

> *This man was handed over to you by God's set purpose and foreknowledge; and you, with the help of wicked men, put him to death by nailing him to the cross.* (Acts 2:23 NIV)

Take note of the phrase, *"God's set purpose and foreknowledge."* God knew that Jesus was going to be crucified. Jesus, too, knew that He was going to be crucified, and He warned His disciples about this many times. (See, for example, Matthew 20:17–19, 26:2; Mark 10:32–34; Luke 18:31–33.) He told them in detail what was going to happen.

But because they did not understand God's wisdom and God's strength—because they still thought like the people of this world and viewed the cross as weakness, foolishness, and defeat—they could not comprehend what Jesus was telling them. It is important for us to remember that the cross is the expression

of God's wisdom and strength; it was the glorious and perfect outworking of His purpose.

There is a beautiful phrase in Revelation 13:8 that describes Jesus as *"the Lamb slain from the foundation of the world."* This shows that the death of Jesus was no accident. In the eyes of the world, it was foolishness and weakness, but for those whose eyes have been opened through the Spirit and the Word of God, it is the height of wisdom and strength.

In his first epistle to the Corinthians, Paul again contrasted the wisdom of this world with the wisdom of God:

> *However, we speak wisdom among those who are mature, yet not the wisdom of this age, nor of the rulers of this age, who are coming to nothing. But we speak the wisdom of God in a mystery, the hidden wisdom which God ordained before the ages for our glory, which none of the rulers of this age knew; for had they known, they would not have crucified the Lord of glory.*
>
> (1 Corinthians 2:6–8)

Paul then quoted the prophet Isaiah:

> *But as it is written, "Eye has not seen, nor ear heard, nor have entered into the*

*heart of man the things which God has
prepared for those who love Him." But
God has revealed these things to us
through His Spirit.*   (verses 9–10)

Speaking again about the cross, Paul said
it is a secret, hidden wisdom that the people
of this world—especially the rulers of this
world—do not understand. The crucifixion
was ordained by God before time began and it
is for our glory. What
a beautiful thought!
Through this secret,
hidden wisdom of
the cross, we can
see what no human
mind could conceive
or imagine and what
human senses can
never discern: what God has prepared for
those who love Him. This is revealed only by
the Holy Spirit and only through the cross.

*God
ordained the
crucifixion
for our
glory.*

The passage above from 1 Corinthians
always excites me because for many years I
was a student—and later a teacher—of philosophy. *Philosophy* means "the love or the
pursuit of wisdom." For many years I pursued
wisdom, but it was only the wisdom of this

world, and it never fully satisfied me. I finally came to realize that there must be something more truly satisfying. Then, when I came to study the Bible and to know Jesus, I discovered that God had prepared this secret, hidden wisdom for His people.

I also discovered that there is only one way to access this secret, hidden wisdom; there is only one door through which we can enter. That door is the cross. It is only as we appropriate by faith what Jesus accomplished for us on the cross, and only as we allow the principle of the cross to be worked out in our own lives, that the secret, hidden wisdom and strength of God become effective in our lives. His wisdom is foolishness to the world; His strength is weakness to the world. And yet God's wisdom is wiser than the world; God's strength is stronger than the world.

CHAPTER TWO

The Measure of True Strength

One of the priceless blessings of the Bible is that it enables us to see this life from God's perspective. God's view of strength and man's view of strength directly oppose one another. This dichotomy naturally leads us to ask, "What is God's standard of strength?"

I believe this question is answered in a verse from Romans where Paul wrote, *"We then who are strong ought to bear with the scruples of the weak, and not to please ourselves"* (Romans 15:1).

When God first opened my eyes to see how He measured strength, it made a profound and lasting impact on me. God taught me that the scriptural mark of strength is not how much you can do but rather how much you can bear of the weaknesses of others. It is satisfying to be strong in your own ability, but that really does not require much spiritual strength.

Spiritual strength is required, however, if you are to bear the weaknesses of others. I believe that spiritual strength is evaluated by God and by the Scriptures as a measure of the degree to which we are able to support other people and bear their weaknesses. For me, this task has never been easy.

Spiritual strength allows us to bear others' weaknesses.

This type of strength and the way in which it is measured is the opposite of the spirit of this age. The spirit of the age proclaims the creed, "Get what you can for yourself. Let the weak take care of themselves."

The challenge to bear the weaknesses of others can be applied to many facets of life, but here we will examine only one of those facets:

the issue of abortion. Abortion is not detestable simply because it constitutes murder (and is thus forbidden by God). No; at its root, the attitude that justifies abortion is completely opposed to Christianity. As Christians, we are not to turn our backs on the weak—to say nothing of disposing of them intentionally.

One of the outstanding marks of Christians in the first century was that they cared for the weak and nursed the sick. They did not write them off, and this impressed the ancient world. Non-Christians could not understand why Christians were concerned about people who had nothing to offer, who were merely liabilities. I believe that writing off humans as liabilities is not strength; rather, it is weakness.

The so-called "liabilities"—the incapacitated, the infirm, the believers who are weak in faith—are the test of our spiritual strength. We cannot permit ourselves to live by the established standards of the age—standards that tell us to put ourselves first and to forget the people who will only drag us down.

For me as a Christian, my first motive is to please Jesus Christ in all that I do. Once we begin to live by seeking to please Jesus, we will inevitably lead lives that are completely different from the lives of others around us who live by the standard of the age.

In Matthew 5:13, Jesus taught that Christians are to be *"the salt of the earth."* I believe that salt serves three practical functions that apply to us as Christians.

First of all, salt purifies and cleanses; it is a mild antiseptic. For example, when your throat is sore, gargling with salt water speeds up the healing process. Saline solutions are used in some medical treatments, and sea salt can help to remove plaque and prevent gingivitis.

> *Christians are to be to society what salt is to food.*

Second, salt is a preservative. In the days before refrigeration, salt was used to cure meat in order to preserve it. Sailors used salt to preserve the meat that sustained them during long voyages at sea. The salt would draw out moisture from the meat, thereby removing what provided a prime breeding ground of bacteria. Thus, salt kept the meat from becoming rotten and corrupted.

Third, salt is added to food to render it palatable and acceptable when it would otherwise be tasteless and unacceptable. As Christians, we are charged to do for our society what salt does in the natural order.

First of all, we are responsible to purify and cleanse our society by our very presence, by our influence, and by our prayers. We are to be a purifying influence that does not go along with the forces of evil but actively resists them.

Second, we are to preserve our society by stopping the forces of corruption that seek to ruin it. Manifest corruption is at work in every area of our lives: social, political, moral, and educational. But we are to be an influence that restrains those forces of corruption and does not allow them free rein.

Third, we are to be to society what salt is to food. We are to make the place in which we find ourselves palatable, acceptable, and appealing to God. We are to render our society acceptable to God by our presence. We are to hold back God's judgment and commend others to His mercy by our presence.

One primary way in which we can do this today is to demonstrate to the world that there is a kind of strength the world knows nothing about—a strength that is not brutal, cruel, or aggressive. This strength does not oppress others but lifts them up; this strength does not exploit and enslave but cares and liberates; this strength does not destroy but heals.

CHAPTER THREE

Exchanging Strength

The strength that this world recognizes is the type exhibited by many political systems and military powers. This type of strength is used to master, control, subjugate, and dominate. It exacts and enforces its own will—a will directed and motivated by selfishness. It is concerned for its own ends rather than for the good of its subjects.

It is significant that in the Bible's prophetic preview of the close of this age, recorded by John in the book of Revelation, various political powers that arise are represented by wild beasts: the lion, the bear, the leopard, and so on. These ferocious animals exhibit the kind of strength that the world values and strives to secure. The book of Revelation indicates that this kind of strength will play an increasingly prominent role in the events that will unfold to bring the age to its close.

Not only does the book of Revelation foretell the coming of the Antichrist and Satan's deception; it also prefigures all of God's purposes being worked out to their triumphant conclusion. Jesus is presented as the sovereign Lord of the universe. The title given Him is *"The Lion of the tribe of Judah"* (Revelation 5:5). But when John actually sees the One so designated, he does not see a lion but a Lamb—a Lamb looking as if it had been slain.

> *But one of the elders said to me, "Do not weep. Behold, the Lion of the tribe of Judah, the Root of David, has prevailed to open the scroll and to loose its seven seals."And I looked, and behold, in the midst of the throne and of the four living creatures, and in the midst of the elders, stood a Lamb as though it had been slain, having seven horns and seven eyes, which are the seven Spirits of God sent out into all the earth.*
>
> (Revelation 5:5–6)

There at the very center of the universe—at the place of ultimate authority and honor—was a Lamb looking as though it had been slain. John expected to see a lion, but what he saw was a slain Lamb. I interpret this as the clearest picture possible to illustrate the difference between the world's view of strength and God's view of strength. The world sees the lion as the epitome of strength and might. God, however, sees a different kind of strength—not in a powerful lion but in a meek, innocent Lamb that has been slain.

God's strength comes to us through the cross.

What God considers strength, the world regards as weakness; what God considers wisdom, the world regards as foolishness. But recall what Paul told us in his first epistle to the Corinthians: *"Because the foolishness of God is wiser than men, and the weakness of God is stronger than men"* (1 Corinthians 1:25).

God's strength comes to us through one channel alone: the cross of Jesus Christ. At the cross, a divinely ordained exchange took place. Jesus, the sinless Son of God, took upon Himself the evil that was due to us, as sinners and rebels, that in return, we might receive the good that Jesus deserved. Jesus died our death that we might have His life. He was made sin that we might be made righteous. He was made a curse that we might receive a blessing. He was wounded that we might be healed.

Jesus died our death that we might have His life.

Through His death on the cross, Jesus was made weakness and foolishness that we might receive, in exchange, the strength and the wisdom of God. Through the cross, God offers us His strength to replace our weakness; His wisdom to replace our foolishness. These benefits come as we wait patiently in faith at the foot of the cross.

The book of Isaiah has a beautiful passage that expresses the difference between natural strength and God's strength and the way that we can exchange our own limited natural strength for the limitless strength of God.

Exchanging Strength

Do you not know? Have you not heard? The Everlasting God, the LORD, the creator of the ends of the earth does not become weary or tired. His understanding is inscrutable. He gives strength to the weary, and to him who lacks might He increases power. Though youths grow weary and tired, and vigorous young men stumble badly, yet those who wait for the LORD will gain new strength; they will mount up with wings like eagles, they will run and not get tired, they will walk and not become weary. (Isaiah 40:28–31 NASB)

In this passage we see the clear contrast between natural strength and divine strength. Natural strength is represented by the youths and the vigorous young men. But their natural strength is not sufficient. *"Though youths grow weary and tired, and vigorous young men stumble badly..."* (verse 30). The lesson here is that natural strength is not sufficient.

There is an alternative to natural strength: as we wait for the Lord, we will gain *"new strength"* (verse 31). The literal translation in Hebrew is, "we will exchange strength." An exchange is what is truly signified here. We

have to come to the end of our own strength; when we do, we give up our own strength, exchanging God's strength for our weakness. When we have come to the end of all that we can do with our own strength, God's strength is made available to us.

Notice what God's strength will do for us: "[we] *will mount up with wings like eagles, [we] will run and not get tired,* [we] *will walk and not become weary"* (Isaiah 40:31). In this verse we find three illustrations of strength. First is the tremendous, surging flight of the eagle that soars high up into the sky, far above all other birds. This flight is majestic and dramatic.

Second is the intense activity: "[we] *will run and not get tired."*

Third is the less intense activity: "[we] *will walk and not become weary."*

Which of these three do you think is the most difficult—to soar, to run, or to walk? Believe me, the most difficult of the three is to walk—the daily, plodding existence that can seem humdrum and monotonous, making us wonder if any part of life is worthwhile.

But as we wait upon God—as we wait at the foot of the cross—we receive strength for all three: to soar, to run, and to walk.

Exchanging Strength

In 2 Corinthians, Paul testified personally how he found strength in his own weakness. Paul was a man who had extraordinary revelations. He received tremendous truth from God that has been a blessing to all Christians of all subsequent ages. But he had to pay a price for it.

> *And lest I should be exalted above measure by the abundance of the revelations, a thorn in the flesh was given to me, a messenger of Satan to buffet me, lest I be exalted above measure. Concerning this thing I pleaded with the Lord three times that it might depart from me. And He said to me, "My grace is sufficient for you, for My strength is made perfect in weakness." Therefore most gladly I will rather boast in my infirmities, that the power of Christ may rest upon me. Therefore I take pleasure in infirmities, in reproaches, in needs, in persecutions, in distresses, for Christ's sake. For when I am weak, then I am strong.*
> (2 Corinthians 12:7–10)

There was some sort of spiritual force at work in Paul's life that was unnatural and demonic; it caused him frequent agony and

tremendous personal problems. Despite this hardship, Paul offered a paradox: *"when I am weak, then I am strong"* (verse 10). In His grace and mercy, God would not lift this pressure that so plagued Paul, for He knew that this pressure drove Paul to the place where he was open to receive God's supernatural strength and power.

When you have come to the end of your own strength—the end of your own wisdom, cleverness, and abilities—God's strength is made available to you. This is a vital secret that each one of us must learn. In our Christian walk, we must arrive at a place where we reach the end of our own strength—where we admit that we are incapable, inadequate, and weak. It is here that, as Isaiah said, God's divine supernatural strength and wisdom are made available to us.

CHAPTER FOUR

The Grain of Wheat

The strength that the world recognizes and values is that of wild beasts—lions, tigers, leopards, and the like. The law of the jungle is the only law known to such strength.

But the strength that comes from God is represented by a Lamb looking as if it had been slain. (See Revelation 5:6.) This Lamb exemplifies two traits that, in the eyes of the world, are the antithesis of strength: meekness and weakness.

This true strength can be released in your life through the daily practice of yielding. Jesus stated this clearly in the Gospel of Luke:

# Gateway to God's Blessing

Then He said to them all, "If anyone desires to come after Me, let him deny himself, and take up his cross daily, and follow Me. For whoever desires to save his life will lose it, but whoever loses his life for My sake will save it."
(Luke 9:23–24)

Here, Jesus established a universal absolute, to which there are no exceptions. If someone decides to follow Jesus, he must do three things: deny himself, take up his cross daily, and then follow Jesus. He has no alternatives.

The third step, actually following Jesus, is impossible until we have taken the first two— learned to deny ourselves and to take up our cross daily.

What does it mean to deny ourselves? The answer is profound in its simplicity. To deny means to say "no." That is Jesus' instruction. We have to say "no" to ourselves.

Inside every one of us is a soul that wants to assert itself. The soul is full of its own wishes, its own desires, its own dissatisfactions. The soul births our base urges and inclinations, which we express along with words such as, "I want," "I think," "I feel," or "I am important."

Our souls demand of other people, "Consult me!" or "Cater to me!" As long as we cede control to our souls, we cannot follow Jesus.

To take the first step and deny ourselves, we must learn to say "no" to our souls. When our souls say, "I want," we need to answer, "What you want isn't important." When our souls say, "I think," we need to answer, "What you think isn't what matters. It is what God says that matters." When our souls say, "I feel," we need to answer, "What you feel isn't important. It is what I believe that matters." There is an answer to silence our souls, and we have to say it.

> *Taking up our crosses means a surrender of our wills.*

After we have said "no" to the selfish soul that inhabits each one of us, we must learn to take up our crosses daily. Taking up our crosses means surrendering our wills—and our claims to our own lives—to the will of God. Jesus came to a place of such surrender in the garden of Gethsemane. He did not take up His physical, wooden cross until He had surrendered His own will to His Father's will.

GATEWAY TO GOD'S BLESSING

In Matthew 26:39, Jesus said, *"O My Father, if it is possible, let this cup pass from Me; nevertheless, not as I will, but as You will."* He said this three times (in verses 39, 42, and 44) until there was nothing else in His mind but to do the will of God at the expense of His own will. Taking up our crosses means doing just as Jesus did. It means saying, "God, not as I will, but as You will."

Jesus knew that He was going to die on the cross. No one imposed that cross upon Him. As He said in the Gospel of John,

> *I lay down My life that I may take it again. No one takes it from Me, but I lay it down of Myself. I have the power to lay it down, and I have the power to take it again.* (John 10:17–18)

Taking up our crosses means that we surrender ourselves voluntarily to God. The order is clear, just as it was in the life of Jesus. At Gethsemane, He prayed to God, *"Not My will, but Yours, be done"* (Luke 22:42). Jesus denied Himself. Then, at Calvary, on the cross, He laid down His life.

Jesus established a pattern that all of His followers must model. They have to deny themselves. They have to follow Him. They have to be willing to die when and where God has appointed for them to reach the end of their earthly lives.

As long as we hold on to our lives, which may seem so precious and exciting, we will not be able to find the lives that God has for us. But if we lose those first lives—if we lay them down—then we will discover another life that God will open up for each one of us. It is a life that is in His will—a life beyond the cross.

In John 12, Jesus used a slightly different illustration to convey this message:

> *Most assuredly, I say to you, unless a grain of wheat falls into the ground and dies, it remains alone; but if it dies, it produces much grain. He who loves his life will lose it, and he who hates his life in this world will keep it for eternal life.* (John 12:24–25)

Jesus used the example of a tiny grain of wheat. As long as that grain remains on its own and stays in the seed basket, it cannot produce any kind of fruit, or life. Jesus said that this grain must fall to the earth and go below the surface. Then, when it is out of sight, concealed in the darkness and dampness of the earth, a change takes place. The hard outer husk rots away, enabling moisture to reach the seed, and a miracle follows as a result: out of that grain that had disappeared and seemed to die, a completely new kind of life springs forth. The green shoot of new life forces its way up through the earth and emerges into the sunlight, and we see a miracle manifest.

This is a picture of what it means to lose our own lives in order to find the lives that God has for us. We come to the end of our own abilities, strength, and wisdom. We let all our own human efforts go; we drop any claims of self-sufficiency.

Then, when the seed has died and the outer husk has rotted away, a new life will come. This is the great challenge that Jesus offered His disciples and continues to offer to us today. We have our own lives; they are in our own hands. As one would grasp a tiny grain of wheat, we can hold on to our lives as long as we like. But as long as we hold on to our lives, they remain isolated and unproductive.

The world is filled with people who are lonely—lonely because they are holding on to their own lives. And yet they won't let go. Jesus says that if we will let go of our lives and surrender to the process of death and suffering, new life will emerge.

The Grain of Wheat

Each of us must take the life that he holds in his hand, release it, and let it go. We must surrender our lives to God. This idea may seem crazy or counterintuitive, but it will yield a completely new life. It is an idea worth pursuing.

CHAPTER FIVE

Those Who Learned to Yield

The principle of yielding—surrendering to the will of God—began long before the times recorded in the New Testament, even though this principle was consummated in the New Testament by Jesus' death on the cross. The practice of the principle of yielding is prominent in the lives of all the servants of God throughout the Bible. Those people who truly found God's purpose for their lives were people who had learned to yield.

Abram

In Genesis 13, Abraham's name was still Abram. He and his nephew, Lot, were shepherds wandering in the land of Canaan—the Land of Promise. They had both become extremely rich, with many servants, flocks, herds, and tents to their name. Their ever-multiplying possessions and ever-growing families made it impossible for one area of land to support both of them, so it became necessary for Abraham and Lot to separate from one another. Their separation is described in Genesis 13:5–11:

> *Lot also, who went with Abram, had flocks and herds and tents. Now the land was not able to support them, that they might dwell together, for their possessions were so great that they could not dwell together. And there was strife between the herdsmen of Abram's livestock and the herdsmen of Lot's livestock. The Canaanites and the Perizzites then dwelt in the land. So Abram said to Lot, "Please let there be no strife between you and me, and between my herdsmen and your herdsmen; for we are brethren. Is not the whole land before you? Please separate from me. If you take the left, then I will go to the right; or, if you go to the right, then I will go to the left." And Lot*

lifted his eyes and saw all the plain of Jordan, that it was well watered everywhere (before the LORD destroyed Sodom and Gomorrah) like the garden of the LORD, like the land of Egypt as you go toward Zoar. Then Lot chose for himself all the plain of Jordan, and Lot journeyed east. And they separated from each other.

The Canaanites and Perizzites were potential enemies, and it was extremely dangerous for God's servants to quarrel among themselves when there were enemies in the land. We Christians would do well to learn to say the same to one another: "Let's not have any quarreling between us, for we are brothers." Abraham is a marvelous example of this. We cannot afford the luxury of quarreling because the enemy is just around the corner and he will exploit any division or disharmony that arises among God's people.

The uncle of Lot, Abraham was the older man. Lot was younger, and in a junior position. Abraham was the spiritual man—the man whom God had chosen to be the father of His special nation that would bring forth the Messiah. It would have been easy for Abraham to say, "I am the senior one; I am the one God has called. The promise is mine. This is what I am going to take; you, Lot, can look after yourself." But Abraham had a different attitude. He humbled himself; he yielded. He said to Lot, "You make the first choice. You take what you want, and I'll take what is left over."

Our submission will release the grace of God.

Abraham demonstrated true humility, the essence of which is to make the right choice without considering the personal cost. If God requires us to submit, the result is not our business. It is God's business. Our submission will release the grace of God into the situation.

Lot went where his soul urged him to go, and it was a bad place: he went toward Sodom. Lot had not learned to say "no" to the demands of his soul as Abraham had.

In Hebrew, the name "Lot" means "a veil, something that covers the eyes." What an apt definition. Lot never discarded the veil of the carnal, self-seeking mind. Although he was a righteous man, he was a carnally righteous man. He did not really have the law of the Spirit in him. But after Lot had parted from Abraham, the veil was removed from Abraham's eyes.

> *And the LORD said to Abram, after Lot had separated from him: "Lift your eyes now and look from the place where you are; northward, southward, eastward, and westward; for all the land which you see I give to you and your descendants forever."*　(Genesis 13:14–15)

As long as Lot was with him, Abraham could not see his inheritance. He was in it, but he could not see it. Abraham had to yield, and yielding brought the revelation. God continued:

> *And I will make your descendants as the dust of the earth; so that if a man could number the dust of the earth, then your descendants also could be numbered. Arise, walk in the land through its length and its width, for I give it to you.*　(verses 16–17)

What Abraham did seemed like foolishness—he gave away the choice land to a younger man who had no legitimate claim. But in doing so, Abraham discovered the key to insight, blessing, and an abundant inheritance.

It is the same with us. Until we learn to yield, we have the veil of the carnal mind over our eyes. We may be in the right position to receive our inheritance, but we will not be able to see it until we have learned to yield.

Jacob

Another example of yielding is seen in the life of Abraham's grandson, Jacob. Like Abraham before him, Jacob was a man of God's choice. Before Jacob and his twin brother, Esau, were born, God had said that Jacob would be the ruler and the leader. (See Genesis 25:23.) But Jacob had to learn the lesson of yielding the hard way. He did not initially have the same humble attitude that Abraham did.

We will not see our inheritance until we learn to yield.

Using his own strength and cleverness, Jacob tried to get what was his by right from

God. First of all, he bought Esau's birthright from him by bribing Esau with a bowl of soup. (See Genesis 25:29–34.) Maybe that was not exactly dishonest, but it certainly was not what you would call brotherly. Jacob was not satisfied with the birthright, however; he wanted his father's blessing. To obtain Isaac's blessing, he cheated by pretending to be Esau. (See Genesis 27:1–29.) He used deceit to receive the blessing, leaving no similar blessing for his older brother, Esau. The name "Jacob" actually means a "cheat" or a "supplanter."

As hard as he tried, Jacob gained nothing worthwhile by cheating. He immediately became a fugitive. Forced to leave the land of his inheritance, he departed and took nothing with him but the staff in his hand.

He spent twenty years in exile, employed by his uncle Laban. Then, after twenty years, the Lord spoke to Jacob and said, *"Return to the land of your fathers and to your family, and I will be with you"* (Genesis 31:3). God said, in essence, "Now is the time to go back to your inheritance!"

So Jacob assembled his wives, children, flocks, herds, and all that he possessed, and headed back toward Canaan, the land of his father. When he reached a certain place on the border of his inheritance, he sent his wives, children, cattle, and everything else on before him, and then he was left alone. That night, a man wrestled with him.

Then Jacob was left alone; and a Man wrestled with him until the breaking of day. Now when He saw that He did not prevail against him, He touched the socket of his hip; and the socket of Jacob's hip was out of joint as He wrestled with him. And He said, "Let Me go, for the day breaks." But he said, "I will not let You go unless You bless me!" So He said to him, "What is your name?" He said, "Jacob." And He said, "Your name shall no longer be called Jacob, but Israel; for you have struggled with God and with men, and have prevailed." Then Jacob asked, saying, "Tell me Your name, I pray." And He said, "Why is it that you ask about My name?" And He blessed him there. So Jacob called the name of the place Peniel: "For I have seen God face to face, and my life is preserved." (Genesis 32:24–30)

The Man Jacob wrestled was no ordinary man. He was what is called a "preincarnate manifestation" of the Son of God—the One who was manifested in history as the Lord Jesus Christ. Man, God, and the messenger from God to man.

Notice the combination of gentleness and power exhibited by the Man with whom Jacob wrestled. Jacob would not give up. Eventually the Man touched the socket of Jacob's hip and put it out of joint, rendering him help-less. There was nothing he could do but plead for mercy.

We must cease to walk in our own strength.

Jacob's story concludes, *"Just as he crossed over Penuel the sun rose on him, and he limped on his hip"* (verse 31).

When Jacob walked with his own strength, he walked out of his inheritance and lost everything. But when he learned to limp, he walked back into his inheritance again.

As long as we trust in our own strength, ability, and cleverness, we remain as Jacob was. We will struggle and strive, but we will not get what God has appointed for us. But when we have a limp—when we no longer walk in our own strength—the way is open for us to walk back into our inheritance. When Jacob did this, he had the blessing of not merely of his father, but also of God.

Jacob had met the Angel—who was God—and received a blessing. But Jacob had to face another encounter: Esau. He heard that Esau was coming to meet him with four hundred armed men, and the last time he had seen Esau, Esau was after his life. I suppose Jacob may have felt more than a little nervous. Let us read Genesis, chapter 33:

> *Now Jacob lifted his eyes and looked, and there, Esau was coming, and with him were four hundred men. So he divided the children among Leah, Rachel, and the two maidservants. And he put the maidservants and their children in front, Leah and her children behind, and Rachel and Joseph last. Then he crossed over before them and bowed himself to the ground seven times, until he came near to his brother.* (Genesis 33:1–3)

Jacob bowed seven times—an act of true humility. In the Bible, the number seven is always an indicator of the Holy Spirit's presence. The Holy Spirit had done some work in Jacob—the man whom God had chosen, the man who had the birthright, the man who had his father's blessing, the man who had an Angel's blessing. When he met Esau, his carnal brother, he bowed seven times. I believe that this act proved that Jacob had the blessing; it was the outworking of what had happened between Jacob and the Angel. Before Jacob met the Angel, he never would have bowed out of his own volition. But having met the Angel, he bowed seven times.

We see the result of Jacob's turnaround in Genesis 33:4: *"But Esau ran to meet him, and embraced him, and fell on his neck and kissed him, and they wept."*

Seemingly unsolvable problems and barriers can often be resolved by humility. James 4:6 says, *"God resists the proud, but gives grace to the humble."* If we want to receive God's grace, we must humble ourselves—before God *and* men.

I once became very angry with one of our daughters, but I was not prepared to change my attitude. As a result, I experienced an odd sensation in my chest—it was almost like a lump or a sort of pressure. Ecclesiastes 7:9 says, *"Anger rests in the bosom of fools."* I carried this pressure around for two days, and I knew there was only one way to get rid of it: I had to go to my daughter and ask her to forgive me. I am glad I did. I believe that if I had failed to ask for forgiveness, the blessing of God would have been withdrawn from my ministry.

There will come situations and problems to which the sole solution is to humble ourselves. We should not expect carnal people to do what spiritual people should do. It is our own responsibility to be spiritual, and to prove that we are indeed so. If you are the spiritual one, prove it. Abraham yielded to a man and Jacob yielded to God. In both cases, yielding opened the way for the revelation and fulfillment of God's purpose. The same is true in our own lives.

CHAPTER SIX

Up Is Down

braham and Jacob yielded in order to receive their inheritance from God. This formula—yielding to receive one's inheritance—could be considered a sort of "spiritual law." We are all familiar with "natural laws" or "scientific laws," such as Sir Isaac Newton's law of universal gravitation. None of us would expect to operate in a way that contradicts the law of gravity.

Many people who are familiar with natural laws have no concept of spiritual laws. But spiritual laws are every bit as definite, precise, and certain as natural laws—and are equally impossible to defy. You cannot break the law

of gravity; you may try, but the law of gravity will only break you.

The same is true of spiritual laws. People talk about breaking God's laws, but that concept is amiss. I want to unfold to you a spiritual law that I believe operates throughout the entire universe. It operated before the universe was created, and I believe it will continue to operate after time is no more. It is a law that affects each one of us, and it has a definite bearing on the course of our lives.

This spiritual law is stated three times in the New Testament—in Matthew 23:12, Luke 14:11, and Luke 18:14—and each time, it comes from the lips of Jesus Himself.

> *And whoever exalts himself will be humbled, and he who humbles himself will be exalted.* (Matthew 23:12)

This law is universal. Anybody anywhere who exalts himself at any time will be humbled. Equally universal is the truth that anyone who humbles himself will be exalted.

There are a number of other passages in Scripture that say the same thing, only with different words. The book of Proverbs mentions it twice, first in chapter 16: *"Pride goes*

before destruction, and a haughty spirit before a fall" (Proverbs 16:18).

People tend to say, "pride goes before a fall." While true in principle, this statement it is not exactly what the Scripture says. In fact, Scripture says something much more sobering: *"Pride goes before destruction."*

The book of Proverbs mentions the danger of pride again in Proverbs 18:12: *"Before destruction the heart of a man is haughty, and before honor is humility."*

I do not believe the downfall of any living creature was ever caused by anything but pride. The first sin in the universe was not drunkenness, immorality, or murder; it was pride. Many people who are horrified by drunkenness, immorality, and murder will tolerate pride, scarcely seeing it as a sin.

> *The first sin in the universe was pride.*

The sin of pride led to rebellion. The inner condition of pride was expressed in the outer action of rebellion. This sin took place not on earth but in heaven. It was committed not by a human being but an angel—Lucifer. The root of Lucifer's pride was the beauty and wisdom that had been imparted to him by the Creator. And yet these gifts ultimately produced rebellion against the very Creator who produced them.

Ezekiel 28 is a prophetic passage in the Old Testament that reveals not merely the future but also sheds light on the past. Sometimes we forget that prophetic insight and ministry are related not only to the future—things we cannot know because they have not yet happened—but also to the past—things we did not know because we were not there and we have no means of knowing except by prophetic revelation.

In this passage in Ezekiel, the prophet speaks of two different individuals related to the city of Tyre. The first person is called *"the prince of Tyre."* The second person is called *"the king of Tyre."* The first person was a human being; the second person most certainly was not:

> *Son of man, say to the prince of Tyre,*
> *"Thus says the Lord GOD: 'Because*
> *your heart is lifted up, and you say,*
> *"I am a god, I sit in the seat of gods,*
> *in the midst of the seas," yet you are*

*a man, and not a god, though you set
your heart as the heart of a god....Will
you still say before him who slays you,
"I am a god"? But you shall be a man,
and not a god, in the hand of him who
slays you."*   (Ezekiel 28:2, 9)

Here is a person who is a man but claims
to be a god. He is the prince, or ruler, of Tyre.
Now we will look at the king of Tyre, who is not
a human being, in verses 11–17:

*Moreover the word of the LORD came
to me, saying, "Son of man, take up a
lamentation for the king of Tyre, and
say to him, 'Thus says the Lord GOD:
"You were the seal of perfection, full of
wisdom and perfect in beauty. You were
in Eden, the garden of God; every precious stone was your covering: the sar-
dius, topaz, and diamond, beryl, onyx,
and jasper, sapphire, turquoise, and
emerald with gold. The workmanship of
your timbrels and pipes was prepared
for you on the day you were created. You
were the anointed cherub who covers; I
established you; you were on the holy
mountain of God; you walked back and
forth in the midst of fiery stones. You*

were perfect in all your ways from the day you were created, till iniquity was found in you. By the abundance of your trading you became filled with violence within, and you sinned; therefore I cast you as a profane thing out of the mountain of God; and I destroyed you, O covering cherub, from the midst of the fiery stones. Your heart was lifted up because of your beauty; you corrupted your wisdom for the sake of your splendor....""" (Ezekiel 28:11–17)

This description is vivid, and it is clear that what it describes is no human being. Verse 12 says that this creature excelled in wisdom and in beauty. In verse 13, we read that this creature had been in Eden, the garden of God.

That takes us right back to Genesis. In verse 14, we find that this creature was *"anointed* [as a] *cherub who covers."* This verse also says, *"You were on the holy mountain of God."* In verse 15, we read, *"You were perfect in all your ways from the day you were created."* So this is a created being—not a man, but a cherub.

Then, in verse 16, it says, *"By the abundance of your trading you became filled with violence within, and you sinned."* And verse 17 identifies the root of the problem: *"Your heart was lifted up because of your beauty; you corrupted your wisdom for the sake of splendor; so I cast you to the ground."*

The word that is translated as *trading* in verse 16 is translated in the King James Version as *traffic*. It is a Hebrew root word whose primary meaning is "to go to and fro, to go backwards and forwards." This word is associated with the practice of trade because a trader is someone who goes to and fro, fetching his wares and selling them at various markets. However, its original meaning is not confined to trade. Leviticus 19 uses a word from the exact same root: *"You shall not go about as a talebearer* [spreading slander] *among your people"* (Leviticus 19:16).

The root concept is "going about" as a talebearer or spreading slander. Then, out of "going about" develops the things that happen when a person does just that. One of them is *trade*, but the one that this passage refers to, which is primary, is *slander*—carrying around tales or spreading untrue reports.

Another example is Proverbs 11:13, which says that *"a talebearer reveals secrets."* That is the basic meaning of the word. Returning to Ezekiel 28:16, we read, *"By the abundance of your trading you became filled with violence within."*

This means that by going about as a slanderer and a talebearer spreading false reports, Lucifer promoted rebellion.

And because of his rebellion, he was cast out from the presence of God. I believe that is the correct picture.

I sometimes wonder if Lucifer said something like this: "You know, you angels, I want you to understand that the Lord [said with rather a cynical tone of voice] does not really appreciate you. You have capabilities. You're capable of more than is being given to you. Now, if you were to follow me, I would see that your full potential was developed. What would you think about setting up our own kingdom? Why should we serve this God? I believe I could make as good a god as the God we serve."

> *Rebellion against God results in dismissal from His presence.*

The amazing thing is that apparently, in the full light of heaven's glory, in a perfect universe that had never been marred by sin, these tactics succeeded! The realization of this fact causes me to tremble, because if Satan's tactics worked in heaven—where sin had never been heard of, let alone perpetrated, and where God was revealed in His glory and beauty—how much more effectively will Satan's tactics work on earth? They have proven to work more effectively for thousands of years.

We need to understand the way Satan operates, because he still operates in the same way he did when he was dismissed from heaven. Revelation 12:4 tells us that Lucifer's pride sparked a rebellion in which one-third of the created angels turned against their Creator, God, and followed Satan instead.

Consider also the tremendous scope of authority that God had delegated to Lucifer. He had granted him authority over one-third of the created angels. When Lucifer fell in rebellion, the entirety of that part of God's kingdom was irrevocably swept away with him. By *irrevocably*, I mean that I do not believe there is any way back for fallen angels; once they are fallen, they are without hope of restoration.

This is a sobering thought indeed. For those of us who are in authority, however small the measure may be, I think we should remind ourselves continually that the effects of our disobedience or disloyalty can have irrevocable effects on those who are under us.

And those who are under authority should examine the authority they are following. It is dangerous to submit to a man who is not submitted to anyone else. I think that this sort of submission, blind and unconditional, is an almost certain road to ultimate disaster.

There is a parallel passage familiar to many that actually uses the name "Lucifer":

How you are fallen from heaven, O Lucifer, son of the morning! How you are cast down to the ground, You who weakened the nations! (Isaiah 14:12)

Prophecy in Scripture reveals not just the outward acts, but also the inner motivation, the essential, inner facts. In Isaiah, we see the motivation that caused Lucifer to rebel: pride. I marvel that God knew what Lucifer was saying in his heart all the time, and that He still let him get away with it. You may think you are getting away with something, but I want to tell you that God knows what you are doing. Even if God lets you get away with it for months, or even years, one day you will discover that God knew all about it.

> *For you have said in your heart: "I will ascend into heaven, I will exalt my throne above the stars of God; I will also sit on the mount of the congregation on the farthest sides of the north; I will ascend above the heights of the clouds, I will be like the Most High." Yet you shall be brought down to Sheol, to the lowest depths of the Pit.*
>
> (Isaiah 14:13–15)

Two words occur five times in the passage above. They are the motivating words of all action: *"I will."* The root problem of the universe is the will of the creature in opposition to the will of the Creator.

1. *"I will ascend into heaven"* (verse 13).

2. *"I will exalt my throne above the stars of God"* (verse 13).

3. *"I will sit on the mount of the congregation"* (verse 13).

4. *"I will ascend above the heights of the clouds"* (verse 14).

5. *"I will be like* [or equal to] *the Most High"* (verse 14). This is the climax.

The Hebrew language has five main verb forms, one of which is used to indicate something that is done repetitively or with special intention. This is the form that is used in this passage. It is not "I will be" but "I will make myself." Satan said, in other words, "It is my aim or my purpose—my ongoing intention and endeavor—to make myself equal to the Most High." The result was Lucifer's fall. Whoever exalts himself will be humbled. This principle never fails.

> *Whoever exalts himself will be humbled.*

God's response to Lucifer's rebellion was something that I believe only He would have thought of. I believe God saw that this issue of pride had to be dealt with in such a way that when it was finished, the problem would never occur again. So God decided to make a new kind of creature, whose name was Adam (or "man"). As I understand Scripture, this creature was made in a way that no other creature had been made.

Up Is Down

Of all the other creatures, the Bible says that God spoke and it was done. With the word of His mouth and His spirit, He created the heavens and their host and all that was in them. But this one creature was different and unique.

> *And the LORD God formed man of the dust of the ground, and breathed into his nostrils the breath of life; and man became a living being.* (Genesis 2:7)

I believe this happened just as it is recorded. I believe God came to earth, stooped down, took some dust, mingled it with water, formed it into clay, and molded the greatest piece of sculpture that the universe had ever seen. It was a perfect body—beautiful, but lifeless.

And then this eternal being—God in person—stooped lower still, put His divine lips against the lips of clay, and breathed into that body the spirit of life. The inbreathed spirit then turned the clay figure into a living soul. The inbreathed breath of almighty God changed that clay body into a living person—man—and man became a living soul.

Genesis 2:7 is the first instance where the word *Jehovah* (or *Yahweh*) is used. All through the first chapter of Genesis, the word is simply *Elohim* (the word for God). But Jehovah is a personal name that identifies God as a person. Likewise, Adam is a personal name, not just a general noun. So at this point in the record of creation, the emphasis is on personality. A personal God created a personal man for the purpose of having personal fellowship.

Notice that God stooped to create man. He went down, not up. God imparted Himself to man and He breathed His own spirit into that body of clay. Within his being, man combines the highest and the lowest elements: one element is from God, the other is from the earth.

This duality may help us understand some of the struggles we go through as human beings made in the image of God. Those high elements and low elements sometimes come into conflict. One part of me wants the things from above; the other part of me wants the things from below! One function of the Bible's record of creation is to explain what we are like and why certain things happen in our lives. I do not believe that any alternative source supplies these answers. Man relates to two worlds: through his spirit, he relates to God; through his body, he relates to this world.

Chapter Seven

God's Purpose for Man

Before the Bible describes the process of creation, it establishes God's purpose for man. In Genesis 1:26, we read,

Then God said, "Let Us make man in Our image, according to Our likeness; let them have dominion over the fish of the sea, over the birds of the air, and over the cattle, over all the earth, and over every creeping thing that creeps on the earth."

In this passage, we see that God's purpose for man explains two of his features. First of all, man was to visibly represent God in a way

that no other creature did. He was to portray the likeness of the Creator. Second, man was to exercise God's authority on His behalf—authority over the whole earth.

As long as man remained dependent on God, he ruled the earth. That seems paradoxical, especially to modern thought. Today, most people think that to rule means to be independent. But in God's eternal provision, man had to remain dependent in order to rule. The moment he ceased to be dependent, he ceased to rule.

Satan's Enmity against Man

Satan harbored especial enmity against man. Remember that "Satan" was not his original name—he was originally Lucifer, the "light bringer." When he transgressed the bounds of his dominion, he forfeited his original identity and became Satan.

The word *Satan* means "the adversary," "the resister," or "the opposer." He is the one who unfailingly opposes God's purposes and God's people. That is why he is our enemy.

Satan harbored enmity against man for two distinct reasons. First of all, man carried in himself the image of God. Satan could not attack God, but he could attack the image of God in man.

This was demonstrated vividly to me many years ago. I knew a young Christian woman who was engaged to a young man, and she carried his photograph everywhere with her. When she discovered that the young man had jilted her, she tore his photograph into tiny pieces. She vented her anger against the young man by marring his image.

> *Satan hates us because we bear the image of God.*

This example provides a better understanding of one of the reasons that Satan hates us: we bear the image of God. Satan cannot attack God, but he can take God's image as it appears in men and defile it, stamp on it, and shake his fist at God. If you see someone who has lost his human dignity, bear in mind that this loss is the work of Satan, who releases his enmity against God on the creatures God made in His likeness.

The second reason for Satan's enmity against man is that man is destined to take the place from which Satan fell. In a sense, man is Satan's rival. In Genesis 3, we learn that Satan instigated man's downfall by his cunning.

> *Now the serpent was more cunning than any beast of the field which the LORD God had made. And he said to the woman, "Has God indeed said, 'You shall not eat of every tree of the garden'?" And the woman said to the serpent, "We may eat of the fruit of the trees of the garden; but of the fruit of the tree which is in the midst of the garden, God has said, 'You shall not eat it, nor shall you touch it, lest you die.'" Then the serpent said to the woman, "You will not surely die. For God knows that in the day you eat of it your eyes will be opened, and you will be like God, knowing good and evil." So when the woman saw that the tree was good for food, that it was pleasant to the eyes, and a tree desirable to make one wise, she took of its fruit and ate. She also gave to her husband with her, and he ate.* (Genesis 3:1–6)

Notice three steps of Satan's deception of man. The first thing he did was question God's word. He asked, *"Has God indeed said...?"* (verse 1).

I believe that Eve lost the battle the moment she entertained that question. Satan's tactics have not changed.

In many churches, people confront one another and ask, "Has God indeed said...?" If we entertain this question, we put ourselves in the same dangerous position that Eve occupied. We cannot afford to entertain the questioning of God's Word.

Second, Satan questioned God's goodness. He said, *"God knows that in the day you eat of it your eyes will be opened, and you will be like God, knowing good and evil"* (verse 5).

The implication is that God is an unjust and arbitrary despot who is keeping His creatures in a lower degree of subjection than they should occupy.

The temptation—the bait Satan offered—was exactly the same motivation that caused his own fall.

He said, *"You will be like God"* (verse 5), or equal with God. He had already made the same claim about himself—*"I will be like the Most High"* (Isaiah 14:14).

Results of Adam's Fall

We learn is Genesis that Adam's fall produced seven consequences:

1. Adam's direct fellowship with God was broken.

2. Adam's source of life was cut off. He was like a battery that would never be recharged. There was a tremendous amount of divine life in him, but it ultimately had to run down.

3. Adam became subject to corruption—sickness, old age, wrinkles, stiff joints, and the like.

4. Adam became subject to satanic harassment. I believe that from then on, he was the victim and object of demonic aggression.

5. Adam became a slave instead of a king. He could have been a king if he had remained dependent, but he chose independence and became a slave. That is true of so many people whom we meet today. Their attitude says, "I don't want to have to obey anybody. Nobody is going to tell me what to do.

I'll be independent." And what do they become? Slaves.

6. Adam's realm became subject to vanity or futility. This is another example of the frightening effects of the misuse of authority. When Lucifer rebelled, a third of the angels fell with him and were implicated in his guilt. The same principle applied to Adam's fall. The entire earth felt the consequences of his disobedience. Thorns and thistles appeared where they had never been before, and everything that is hard and unpleasant, anything that causes strain, anything that demands labor, and anything that produces frustration came into this earth through the disobedience of Adam.

7. Adam became identified with Satan in the guilt of rebellion—he became a rebel like Satan. This is a crucial fact because it took the wisdom of God to find the solution and to dissolve this association and its fatal consequences.

Many people often wonder why God does not simply destroy Satan. I believe it is because of

His mercy toward the human race. Satan—in his cunning—got the human race involved in the same guilt in which he was involved. I can imagine Satan saying something like, "All right, God, I am a rebel. I know it and You know it; there is no question about it. And that lake of burning fire over there is where I am headed. We both know it, and You can send me there at any time. But listen, You are a just God, so You cannot compromise Your justice. These human beings are rebels, just like me. So the day You send me to the burning lake of fire, You must send the human beings there, too."

The lower we go, the higher we get.

If this hypothetical dialogue occurred and Satan so challenged God, he clearly did not know that God had an answer for him even before he posed the challenge.

Man Redeemed

In order to redeem the fallen human race, God stooped lower still. The lower we go, the higher we get. But every time we go higher, we end up lower. In the person of Jesus Christ, God identified Himself with the fallen race and made amends for its guilt.

And once its guilt was expunged, He did not need to compromise His justice to consign Satan to the place where he belonged, while simultaneously offering mankind a means of escaping the same fate.

In Romans 3:26, Paul wrote that God sent His Son, Jesus Christ, to die for our sins, *"that He might be just and the justifier of the one who has faith in Jesus."* That was the problem. How could God forgive without compromising His justice? How could He spare man and still consign Satan to his well-deserved end? The answer is: through Jesus.

> *Since the children have flesh and blood, he too shared in their humanity so that by his death he might destroy him who holds the power of death—that is, the devil—and free those who all their lives were held in slavery by their fear of death.* (Hebrews 2:14–15 NIV)

Jesus not only created Adam, but by redemption, He also identified Himself in His own person with Adam and the fallen human race. In doing so, He became the expiation for our sins.

> *Christ...Himself bore our sins in His own body on the tree, that we, having died to sins, might live for righteousness—by whose stripes you were healed....For Christ also suffered once for sins, the just for the unjust, that He might bring us to God.*
>
> (1 Peter 2:21, 24; 3:18)

Here we see the true essence of the cross: the sinless Son of God became identified with the sinful, fallen human race. As our representative, He took our guilt upon Him, paid our full penalty, and was raised again from the dead, thereby making it possible for God to both forgive us and judge Satan without compromising His justice.

The plan of redemption goes one amazing step further. Not only did Jesus identify Himself with us, but through our faith, we become identified with Him.

The lowest are raised to the highest. If we want to go up, we must go down.

God not only took a creature formed of dust, but God took that creature—depraved, corrupted, and fallen—and offered him the highest place in the universe.

> *But God, who is rich in mercy, because of His great love with which He loved us, even when we were dead in trespasses, made us alive together with Christ (by grace you have been saved), and raised us up together, and made us sit together in the heavenly places in Christ Jesus.* (Ephesians 2:4–6)

This passage describes our identification with Jesus. Everything that Jesus went through, we are invited to join Him in going through. First of all, we have to identify ourselves with Him in His death. We reckon ourselves dead. We are identified with Him in His burial by our baptism.

Through our faith, we are identified with Jesus.

And having been identified with Him in death and burial, we are identified with Him in three additional phases: we are made alive with Him, we are resurrected with Him, and we are enthroned with Him.

Gateway to God's Blessing

God absolutely, specifically, and literally took the lowest, and, in Christ, raised it to the highest to seat us with Him on the throne of the universe.

Furthermore, God will use these fallen but redeemed creatures to demonstrate forever this law to the universe.

Paul revealed this ultimate purpose in Ephesians 1:

For he chose us in him before the creation of the world to be holy and blameless in his sight. In love he predestined us to be adopted as his sons through Jesus Christ, in accordance with his pleasure and will—to the praise of his glorious grace, which he has freely given us in the One he loves. In him we have redemption through his blood, the forgiveness of sins, in accordance with the riches of God's grace that he lavished on us with all wisdom and understanding. And he made known to us the mystery of his will according to his good pleasure, which he purposed in Christ, to be put into effect when the times will have reached their fulfillment—to bring all things in heaven and

on earth together under one head, even
Christ. (Ephesians 1:4–10 NIV)

It is God's *"good pleasure"* (verse 9) to bring
all things in heaven and earth together under
one Head, Jesus Christ. Here is where we come
in. Think of that glorious plan, unfolded from
eternity to eternity.

Paul continued,

In him we were also chosen, having
been predestined according to the plan
of him who works out everything in
conformity with the purpose of his will,
in order that we, who were the first to
hope in Christ, might be for the praise
of his glory. (verses 11–12 NIV)

We—you and I, the human race—are the
number one manifestation of the principle that
if we exalt ourselves, we will be humbled, but
if we humble ourselves, we will be exalted.

Paul made this point again in Ephesians:

And God raised us up with Christ
and seated us with him in the heav-
enly realms in Christ Jesus, in order
that in the coming ages he might show
the incomparable riches of his grace,

expressed in his kindness to us in Christ Jesus. (Ephesians 2:6–7 NIV)

We are the primary demonstration piece of God's grace.

His intent was that now, through the church, the manifold wisdom of God should be made known to the rulers and authorities in the heavenly realms, according to his eternal purpose which he accomplished in Christ Jesus our Lord. (Ephesians 3:10–11 NIV)

It is remarkable to know that for all eternity, we are to be the supreme demonstration to the whole universe of God's wisdom. God took us from the scrap heap and made us into His masterpiece.

CHAPTER EIGHT

Down Is Up

After he rebelled against God and was cast down from heaven, Lucifer's name was changed to Satan. Instead of being the son of the dawn (the one who brings light, the one who heralds the dawn), he became Satan (the resistor, the adversary, the one who opposes God's purposes and God's people). He is an example of the negative aspect of the truth that *"whoever exalts himself will be humbled"* (Matthew 23:12).

Let us explore the positive aspect of that truth, expressed in the second half of the verse: *"he who humbles himself will be exalted"* (Matthew 23:12). The most perfect contrast in this respect is between Lucifer (who became

Satan) and Jesus (who was and is by nature the Son of God, God Himself). Satan reached up but slipped and fell; Jesus stooped down and was lifted up.

If we can focus on those two beings, we will see the most perfect illustration of this truth. But the truth applies in every area of every life, in every time and situation. The way up is down.

In Philippians 2, Paul exhorted believers to align themselves with Christ's perspective:

Your attitude should be the same as that of Christ Jesus: who, being in very nature God, did not consider equality with God something to be grasped, but made himself nothing, taking the very nature of a servant, being made in human likeness. And being found in appearance as a man, he humbled himself and became obedient to death— even death on a cross! Therefore, God exalted him to the highest place and gave him the name that is above every name, that at the name of Jesus every knee should bow, in heaven and on earth and under the earth, and every

*tongue confess that Jesus Christ is
Lord, to the glory of God the Father.*
(Philippians 2:5–11 NIV)

Paul made the observation that Christ's
attitude is in direct opposition to that of Satan,
who *did* consider equality with God something
to be grasped. Satan reached up, grasped for
it, slipped, and fell—irrevocably.

Where the *New International Version* says
Jesus *"humbled himself"* (verse 9), the *New
American Standard Bible* says that Jesus
"emptied Himself" (verse 7), which is a more
literal translation of what happened. "And
Can It Be," one of the great hymns of Charles
Wesley, says, "He emptied Himself of all but
love."

Paul wrote his letter to the Philippians
while in prison. I suppose he did not have any
particular comforts or conveniences, and one
of the things that causes me to marvel at the
inspiration of Scripture is the perfect balance
of this passage—a balance Paul probably did
not premeditate. He may not even have been
conscious of what he wrote. In this passage, we
can identify seven steps down and seven steps
up. In Scripture, seven is often the number

signifying completion, or perfection. It is also associated with the Holy Spirit.

Jesus' Seven Steps Down

1. He emptied Himself, laying aside all the attributes of divinity.

2. He took the form of a servant. He who was the Lord became the servant.

3. He was made in human likeness; He became a man, not an angel.

4. He was found in appearance as a man. When Jesus walked the streets of His hometown, Nazareth, there was nothing special or externally obvious to distinguish Him from all the other people of the town. When Peter ultimately identified Him as the Messiah and the Son of God, Jesus said, *"flesh and blood has not revealed this to you"* (Matthew 16:17). There was nothing in His external appearance to make Him different from the other men of His day.

5. He humbled Himself. Not only was He a man of His time, but He was a humble

man of His time. He was not a prince, a wealthy man, a political leader, or a military commander. He had none of those aspects or functions that tend to impress people in the natural.

6. He became obedient to death. He not only lived as a man, but He died as a man, too.

7. He died on a cross—the ultimate instrument of humiliation, shame, rejection, and agony.

Jesus took seven steps down to the lowest place of all—the place of the criminal. He was rejected by men and even rejected by God the Father on our account.

Philippians 2:9 begins with the word *"therefore."* That is because this is the outworking of a divine law, not just an accident.

Jesus was not exalted because He was God's Son; He was exalted because He earned exaltation.

Even Jesus was subject to this law. There is no one in the universe who is not subject to this law. Whoever humbles himself will be exalted.

Jesus' Seven Steps Up

1. God exalted Him to the highest place.

2. God gave Him the name that is above every name. There is only one name that is above every name, and that is the name of Jesus.

3. At the name of Jesus, every knee should bow. Steps four, five, and six are the different areas of the universe in which knees will bow.

4. *"In heaven."*

5. *"On earth."*

6. *"Under the earth."* The three great areas of the universe are all going to acknowledge the exaltation of Jesus by bowing at the knee.

7. Finally, every tongue should confess that Jesus Christ is Lord, to the glory of God the Father.

Jesus took seven steps down and seven steps up, but He had to do so in that order. He could not take the steps up until He had taken the steps down.

Down Is Up

Meditate on the word *"therefore"* in verse 9: *"**Therefore**, God exalted him to the highest place";* He gave Him the highest place in the universe.

For many years, I thought that it had all been worked out in advance. I assumed that Jesus was just going to do certain things and that God would automatically exalt Him. But I came to realize that I was mistaken. Jesus had to meet certain conditions in order to be exalted. If *He* was required to meet them, believe me, you and I will be required to meet them, too!

Paul introduced the passage in Philippians 2 by establishing that our attitudes should be the same as that of Christ Jesus. He went on to describe this attitude: being willing to go down—and down, and down.

Verse 12, which is the application to our lives, also begins with the word *"therefore."* *Therefore* it is going to work for you and me. It worked in Jesus, so it will work in us. The same attitude that was in Jesus has to be in us. Philippians 2:12–13 reads,

> *Therefore, my dear friends, as you have always obeyed—not only in my presence, but now much more in my*

> *absence—continue to work out your*
> *salvation with fear and trembling, for it*
> *is God who works in you to will and to*
> *act according to his good purpose.*
>   (Philippians 2:12–13 NIV)

The humility of verse 8 leads to the obedience of verse 12. Pride, on the other hand, leads to disobedience; it was the source of Satan's rebellion. The working out of our salvation *"with fear and trembling"* is the working out of the principle that we have to humble ourselves in order to be exalted. Paul described what kind of conduct and nature this humbling will produce:

> *Do everything without complaining or*
> *arguing, so that you may become blame-*
> *less and pure, children of God without*
> *fault in a crooked and depraved gen-*
> *eration, in which you shine like stars in*
> *the universe as you hold out the word*
> *of life—in order that I may boast on the*
> *day of Christ that I did not run or labor*
> *for nothing.*   (Philippians 2:14–16 NIV)

The spiritual man praises; the carnal man complains. Bear in mind that we never can be right with God when we are complaining.

Down Is Up

When we complain, we are not blameless and pure; we can, however, become blameless and pure.

We live in a crooked and depraved generation, but our responsibility is to be the children of God without fault in such a generation. If we are going to shine, one of the things we have to do is to *"hold out the word of life"* (verse 16). We cannot live self-contained, self-pleasing, self-

> *The spiritual man praises; the carnal man complains.*

sufficient lives and ignore the needs of the world if we expect to shine. Shining involves holding out the word of life to those who have not yet received it.

Paul's closing thought is a solemn one: Is what I am doing worthwhile? Paul said, in essence, "If I don't produce this in you, then all the labor that I bestowed on you is in vain."

That is a solemn thought indeed. It is possible for a man to spend his whole life in ministry to people, but if he does not produce the right kind of people, his life's work has been in vain.

When I was a young preacher, I was mainly concerned about what I preached. As I matured, however, I became more concerned about what I was producing, because *"a tree is known by its fruit"* (Matthew 12:33). Good sermons and good programs are of little value if they do not produce good people.

Humility

One fruit that we should hope to produce is humility. Rather than being an emotion or a pious feeling, humility is a decision of the will, and it has to be worked out in action. Many people have the wrong idea about humility. They walk into church on Sunday mornings and think, *Am I feeling humble?* Do not bother about *feeling* humble; just decide to *be* humble. Make the decision.

Humility is a decision of the will.

You hear people pray from time to time, "God, make me humble." I question whether God can do that. I think there is only one person who can make you humble, and that is you. If you do not decide to do it, it will not happen.

Down Is Up

James and Peter made the same point in their epistles.

Humble yourselves before the Lord, and he will lift you up. (James 4:10 NIV)

Young men, in the same way be submissive to those who are older. All of you, clothe yourselves with humility toward one another, because, "God opposes the proud but gives grace to the humble."
(1 Peter 5:5–6 NIV)

Notice that this verse says *"humble **yourselves**." You* do it. In the passage from 1 Peter, we see that there is a certain obligation on those who are young to show respect and submission toward those who are older. But the application does not stop there. Rather, the principle is applied to all of us, young and old alike, with the words, *"clothe yourselves with humility toward one another"* (verse 5).

God opposes the proud but gives grace to the humble. If we want grace, we must humble ourselves. But if we come to God with pride, the Bible says that God knows the proud from afar (Psalm 138:6), and that is where He keeps them. Pride will never gain us access to the presence of God.

Gateway to God's Blessing

Humble yourselves, therefore, under God's mighty hand, that he may lift you up in due time. (1 Peter 5:6 NIV)

It is God who determines the time when we will be lifted up. Jesus did not raise Himself from the tomb; no, He waited for His Father to do it. One of the biggest tests in our lives is humbling ourselves and waiting for God to respond. He usually does not respond when we think He ought to.

For it is commendable if a man bears up under the pain of unjust suffering because he is conscious of God. But how is it to your credit if you receive a beating for doing wrong and endure it? But if you suffer for doing good and you endure it, this is commendable before God. To this you were called, because Christ suffered for you, leaving you an example, that you should follow in his steps. (1 Peter 2:19–21 NIV)

What a beautiful translation. Why should we bear up under the pain of unjust suffering? We will endure it if we are *"conscious of God"* (verse 19).

Down Is Up

Many Christians never realize that unjust suffering is part of their calling. As Christians, we are called to suffer unjustly. Why? To cultivate humility. God will arrange the circumstances; we need to be open to them to see what God is doing.

Humility ultimately must come through a decision of the will. And that decision has to be worked out in actions, not in words or emotions.

Christians are called to suffer unjustly.

Jesus said in Luke 14:8–11 that if someone is invited to a wedding feast, he should not sit at the highest table, but ought to seat himself at the lowest table. Then, the only way to go is up; one cannot help but improve his status.

I love the words of John Bunyan in his poem, "The Shepherd's Song": "He that is down need fear no fall;/ he that is low, no pride;/ he that is humble ever shall/ Have God to be his guide."

One can go no lower than the floor. If we are there already, there is only one way that we can go, and that is up.

When the Bible says, *"humble yourselves before the Lord"* (James 4:10 NIV), it refers to a personal relationship with the Lord.

I have found that one of the best things to do is to get on the floor before the Lord. Sometimes I would lie there on my face and say to Him, "Lord, I want You to know that I know that this is where I belong." And then I would wait there until I felt a release in my spirit from the Lord.

Practical Application

There are two practical ways in which this principle of humbling ourselves has to be applied in our lives.

The first is when we come to God for the first time, and the second is as we progress and mature in the spiritual life.

> *At that time the disciples came to Jesus and asked, "Who is the greatest in the kingdom of heaven?" He called a little child and had him stand among them. And he said: "I tell you the truth, unless you change and become like little children, you will never enter the kingdom of heaven. Therefore, whoever humbles*

himself like this child is the greatest in
the kingdom of heaven."

(Matthew 18:1–4 NIV)

What is there about a child that is humble?
Children are not always entirely sweet in their
behavior; they can be quite ornery or quar-
relsome, but they *are* teachable. They do not
have a lot of hang-ups, preconceptions, or
prejudices.

I believe that this is what Jesus meant
when He said that if we come to God desiring
to enter the kingdom of heaven, we must come
as little children. There is no other way.

In 1 Corinthians, Paul described the kind
of people who belonged to the Corinthian
church:

> *Brothers, think of what you were when*
> *you were called. Not many of you were*
> *wise by human standards; not many*
> *were influential; not many were of*
> *noble birth. But God chose the foolish*
> *things of the world to shame the wise;*
> *God chose the weak things of the world*
> *to shame the strong. He chose the lowly*
> *things of this world and the despised*
> *things—and the things that are not—to*

nullify the things that are, so that no
one may boast before him.
(1 Corinthians 1:26–29 NIV)

There is nothing wrong with being wise, influential, or of noble birth; alone, these qualities are not problematic.

A problem does arise, however, when these qualities produce pride in those who possess them. This happens often. Wisdom is not the problem, but the pride that comes from wisdom is. Noble birth is not the problem, but the pride that comes from noble birth is. This explains why, in the fellowship of believers, the people who possess such qualities are few. It is not as if God were opposed to wisdom, influence, or noble birth, but He is opposed to the tendency of those things to create a barrier of pride in the people who possess them.

All pride must be eradicated. And God made His choice on that basis. Luke addressed this universal principle perhaps more than any of the other Gospel authors:

A certain ruler asked him, "Good
teacher, what must I do to inherit eternal
life?" "Why do you call me good?" Jesus
answered. "No one is good—except God
alone. You know the commandments:

Down Is Up

'Do not commit adultery, do not murder, do not steal, do not give false testimony, honor your father and mother.'" "All these I have kept since I was a boy," he said [and I believe he was speaking the truth]. *When Jesus heard this, he said to him, "You still lack one thing. Sell everything you have and give to the poor, and you will have treasure in heaven. Then come, follow me." When he heard this, he became very sad, because he was a man of great wealth.*

(Luke 18:18–23 NIV)

This man's response is not typical of people who are wealthy, but in the presence of Jesus Christ, his values changed—suddenly and radically.

Jesus looked at him and said, "How hard it is for the rich to enter the kingdom of God! Indeed, it is easier for a camel to go through the eye of a needle than for a rich man to enter the kingdom of God." (verses 24–25 NIV)

The significance of the phrase *"the eye of a needle"* requires an explanation. In Jerusalem, there was a great iron door that closed the Jaffa

Gateway to God's Blessing

Gate to the Old City. The great iron door was closed every night when the sun set. If a traveler came on a camel after dark and sought entry to the city, those responsible would not open the great iron door, but instead would open a smaller iron door cut out from the larger door. This smaller door measured about four feet high and two feet wide. In order to pass through, a visitor would dismount, strip his camel of all the baggage it was bearing, and coax the bare camel to its knees so it could just squeeze through the door. This tiny door was known as the "Needle's Eye."

So when Jesus spoke about a camel going through the *"eye of the needle,"* He was not using some extravagant or irrelevant expression. Rather, He was speaking about something vivid and familiar to his audience. Jesus said that a rich man who desires to come to God must come as a camel would enter the Needle's Eye.

First, he must be stripped of everything—all of his earthly belongings and possessions.

Second, he must get down on his knees. Only by doing these things can he barely squeeze through; there is no room for pride or possessions in that narrow doorway.

Naaman's Humility

The Old Testament includes a story of a man who thought he could come to God in a big way. This was the subject of a sermon I heard when I first got in touch with Pentecostal people. It was a tremendously anointed message about Naaman.

Now Naaman was commander of the army of the king of Aram. He was a great man in the sight of his master and highly regarded, because through him the Lord had given victory to Aram. He was a valiant soldier, but he had leprosy. (2 Kings 5:1 NIV)

How numerous are the people whose descriptions are qualified with a "but." Naaman had everything, *"but...."* He was a commander of the army; he was highly regarded as a valiant soldier—*but* he had this horrible, unclean, incurable disease: leprosy.

He had in his home a little Jewish girl who had been taken captive by the Syrian band, and she was really a model of God's grace. Instead of resenting those who had taken her captive, she was concerned about them.

GATEWAY TO GOD'S BLESSING

She said to her mistress, "If only my master would see the prophet [speaking about Elisha] who is in Samaria! He would cure him of his leprosy." Naaman went to his master and told him what the girl from Israel had said. "By all means, go," the king of Aram replied. "I will send a letter to the king of Israel." So Naaman left, taking with him ten talents of silver, six thousand shekels of gold and ten sets of clothing. (2 Kings 5:3–5 NIV)

Naaman came to God in a big way. In contemporary currency, Naaman took with him more than $250,000 in gold and silver. It was a vast sum of wealth. Naaman brought a letter to the king of Israel that read:

With this letter I am sending my servant Naaman to you so that you may cure him of his leprosy.

(2 Kings 5:6 NIV)

There is an element of humor in this story. The king of Israel was appalled, and he exclaimed, in essence, "What can I do?" Distraught, he even tore his clothes! He thought that the king of Aram was just trying to provoke a quarrel with him.

Down Is Up

When Elisha the man of God heard that the king of Israel had torn his robes, he sent him this message: "Why have you torn your robes? Have the man come to me and he will know that there is a prophet in Israel." So Naaman went with his horses and chariots and stopped at the door of Elisha's house.

(2 Kings 5:8–9 NIV)

What do you think Elisha did? Did he say, "Come in, you are welcome! Take a seat"? No. Elisha did not even go to the door! God, working through Elisha, dealt with the problem of pride in Naaman.

Elisha sent a messenger to say to him, "Go, wash yourself seven times in the Jordan, and your flesh will be restored and you will be cleansed." But Naaman went away angry and said, "I thought that he would surely come out to me and stand and call on the name of the LORD his God, wave his hand over the spot and cure me of my leprosy. Are not Abana and Pharpar, the rivers of Damascus, better than any of the waters of Israel? Couldn't I wash in

them and be cleansed?" So he turned and went off in a rage.

(2 Kings 5:10–12 NIV)

Naaman was like so many of us. He had God preprogrammed, certain that God would cure him and convinced that he knew how this was going to happen. When things did not go as he had expected, he went away angry after taking one look at the Jordan River.

> *There is no such thing as partial obedience.*

Now the Jordan River is not beautiful but muddy. I was baptized in the Jordan River, and when I stood there in the water, I sank in, ankle-deep in this liquid mud on the river bottom. So I can empathize with Naaman's reaction of repugnance.

Naaman's servants went to him and said, "My father, if the prophet had told you to do some great thing, would you not have done it? How much more then, when he tells you, 'Wash and be cleansed'!" (2 Kings 5:13 NIV)

Down Is Up

If Elisha had required a fee that would take all of Naaman's gold and silver, he would not have hesitated to pay it. The trouble was that it was too easy, too simple. And it still is for many people today. But thank God that Naaman had the sense to listen to his servants. He was beginning to learn about true humility.

> *So he went down and dipped himself in the Jordan seven times, as the man of God had told him, and his flesh was restored and became clean like that of a young boy.* (2 Kings 5:14 NIV)

Think of what is involved. Naaman is sporting all his military finery—his four stars, his epaulets, and his medals—and he has to take them all off! What is below the surface? Leprosy. He had to reveal it to his servants, to the people standing on the bank...to everybody.

There is no such thing as partial obedience. Naaman was told to dip himself seven times in the Jordan River. What do you suppose would have happened if Naaman had quit after five times? My personal conviction is that nothing changed until he dipped the

seventh time. After the seventh dip, everything changed. When God says *seven times*, He does not mean six or eight; He means just what He says.

Humility's Role

Humbling ourselves applies particularly in the area of leadership. The paramount qualification for leadership in the church of Jesus Christ is the willingness to humble oneself.

Matthew chapter 20 helps us see this.

Then the mother of Zebedee's sons came to Jesus with her sons and, kneeling down, asked a favor of him. "What is it you want?" he asked. She said, "Grant that one of these two sons of mine may sit at your right and the other at your left in your kingdom" [that is a pretty simple request]. *"You don't know what you are asking," Jesus said to them. "Can you drink the cup I am going to drink?" "We can," they answered* [but they did not know what they were saying]. *Jesus said to them, "You will indeed drink from my cup, but to sit at my right or left is not for me to grant. These places belong to those for whom they have been prepared by my Father." When the ten heard about this, they were indignant with the two brothers. Jesus called them together and said, "You know that the rulers of the Gentiles lord it over them, and their high officials exercise authority over them. Not so with you. Instead, whoever wants to become great among you must be your servant, and whoever wants to be first must be your slave—just as the Son of Man did not come to be served, but to serve, and to give his life as a ransom for many."*

(Matthew 20:20–28 NIV)

The mother of Zebedee's sons was kneeling down, but she was not very humble. There are many outward acts and postures that might suggest humility, but humility is an inward condition; it is an attitude of the heart.

Jesus says the Son of Man came to serve, not to be served. Again, the rule of the kingdom is that if we want to go up, we go down. The further down we go, the higher up we come.

# GATEWAY TO GOD'S BLESSING

And this process is progressive. We come into the kingdom by humbling ourselves, but once we have entered the kingdom, we must go down if we desire promotion. We become the servants of all.

This rule applies for the duration of the Christian life. I doubt whether anyone can truly be a blessing as long as he is not willing to humble himself. As long as we refuse to humble ourselves, our pride stands in the way of the blessings that God wants us to be. Let us look at the example of Paul:

> *To keep me from becoming conceited because of these surpassingly great revelations, there was given me a thorn in my flesh, a messenger of Satan, to torment me. Three times I pleaded with the Lord to take it away from me. But he said to me, "My grace is sufficient for you, for my power is made perfect in weakness." Therefore I will boast all the more gladly about my weaknesses, so that Christ's power may rest on me. That is why, for Christ's sake, I delight in weaknesses, in insults, in hardships, in persecutions, in difficulties. For when I am weak, then I am strong.*
>
> (2 Corinthians 12:7–10 NIV)

Down Is Up

God loves His people so much that He will do everything He possibly can to keep them from becoming proud. Sometimes the issues to which we might object and about which we complain to God are the evidence of His love and concern for us.

Some people believe that the prayers of a spiritual person will always receive answers. By that standard, the apostle Paul was not a spiritual person! He prayed three times and received no answer. When he finally received an answer, it was "no." Some people do not realize that "no" is also an answer.

If we desire God's power, we must remember that it will be manifested in our weaknesses. Paul then reached a *"therefore."* Why should he delight in weakness, in insults, in hardships, in persecutions? Because they humbled him; they brought him lower. He said, in essence, "Every time I go down, I get more of God; when I am weak, then I am strong; when I boast of my infirmities, God's glory rests on me. But when I rely on my own ability, cleverness, experience, and strength, then God withdraws."

John the Baptist made this point most succinctly in John 3:30. Speaking about his relationship with Jesus, the Messiah, for whom he had come to prepare the way, he said, *"He must become greater; I must become less"* (NIV). That simple statement illustrates a progression: to become ever less so that Jesus may become ever greater.

Evangelist Dwight L. Moody once said that as a young man in the service of the Lord, he imagined that God had His gifts stored on shelves. He figured that the best gifts were stored on the top shelves so that one had to reach up to get them. But later on, he revised this image, figuring instead that the best gifts were on the lowest shelves—one had to stoop down to get them.

This principle of humbling ourselves for promotion goes one step further. We have to apply the principle not only in our relationship with God, but also in our relationships with other people. It does not work with God if it does not work with people.

A valid test of where we are in our relationship with God involves evaluating the way we relate to other people. This truth applies to humility as much as any other aspect of the Christian life.

Do nothing out of selfish ambition or vain conceit, but in humility consider

others better than yourselves.
(Philippians 2:3 NIV)

*Submit to one another out of reverence
for Christ.* (Ephesians 5:21 NIV)

We prove the authenticity of our reverence for Christ when we submit to one another. If we claim to be submitted to God but we refuse to submit to other people, we are deceiving ourselves. The evidence of our submission to God consists of our attitude and relationship to other people.

CHAPTER NINE

Do We Fear the Lord?

The title of this chapter poses an important question, one to which many Christians today probably give little thought. It is, however, an extremely important issue—one that we ignore to our own detriment. The Bible has a good deal to say about the fear of the Lord, but great numbers of Christians misunderstand this concept.

Of all the themes in Scripture, the fear of the Lord contains some of the most outstanding promises of God's favor and blessing. In fact, I know of no other theme of Scripture that has more blessings to offer than the fear of the Lord.

Isaiah 33:6 ends with eight little words: *"The fear of the LORD is His treasure."* The fear of the Lord is not something to be afraid of or to despise. Rather, it is God's treasure that He is sharing with His people.

I once asked myself, *Why was that jewel of truth tacked on at the end of a verse in Isaiah?* I came to the conclusion that it was tacked on so subtly because God wants us to *search* for truth. Jesus said that we should search the Scriptures, for in them we will find the truth about Him. (See John 5:39.) Are you one of those people who search the Scriptures? Do you really turn to the Bible with a diligent quest for truth? Do you look to God's Word for answers to your needs and solutions to your problems? Many people are afraid of what God might say to them, but they do not need to be.

> *The fear of the LORD is clean, enduring forever.* (Psalm 19:9)

The fear of the Lord is not merely clean, it is cleansing—it purifies us and keeps us clean. Psalm 19 says that it endures forever—not for this life only, but for eternity. The fear of the Lord will always be a mark of all the true people of God, whether human or angelic.

Do not let your heart envy sinners, But be zealous for the fear of the LORD all the day. (Proverbs 23:17)

Psalm 19 says *"forever"* (verse 9); Proverbs 23 says *"all the day"* (verse 17). In other words, there should never be a time when we are not practicing the fear of the Lord.

What the Fear of the Lord Is *Not*

There are specific forms of fear that are not related to what the Bible means when it speaks of the fear of the Lord.

Natural Fear

I have been told that a newborn baby is naturally afraid of only two things: loud noise and the sensation of falling. As we grow and go forward in life, we make additions to the list of things we naturally fear—roller coasters, wars, getting lost in the dark. These types of fear are perfectly normal. All human beings have these natural fears, but these fears do not constitute what the Bible calls the fear of the Lord.

Demonic Fear

There is also demonic fear. In his second letter to Timothy, Paul wrote,

*For God has not given us a spirit of fear
[or timidity], but of power and of love
and of a sound mind.*   (2 Timothy 1:7)

I would suggest that demonic fear has three marks that distinguish it from the fear of the Lord. First, demonic fear proceeds from Satan, not from God.

Second, demonic fear tends to keep us from obeying God. Satan injects this kind of fear into us to keep us from doing the things God wants us to do. In this way, it is completely opposite of the fear of the Lord, which motivates and impels us to obey God and to do the things that God wants us to do.

Third, demonic fear is tormenting.

*There is no fear in love; but perfect love
casts out fear, because fear involves
torment.*   (1 John 4:18)

There are many examples of demonic fear. One is claustrophobia, or the abnormal fear of being in tight spaces, such as closets or elevators. For many years, my wife Lydia had a fear of getting on an elevator. She would rather walk up six flights of stairs than take the elevator.

Do We Fear the Lord?

One day, God showed us that this phobia was demonic. We said a prayer against her fear, and she was delivered from it, never again to experience problems when getting on an elevator.

Such a phobia is not the fear we are talking about when we discuss the fear of the Lord. Tormenting fear is from the devil, and it has no place in the life of a Christian. It is a kind of fear that is caused by an evil spirit. It is unnatural; it is an excessive reaction. It is something that overpowers us, something we cannot master. It takes control in certain situations, and it is not the fear of the Lord. In fact, the greatest remedy for the tormenting type of fear is the true fear of the Lord.

Religious Fear

The prophet Isaiah wrote about religious fear:

> *Therefore the* Lord *said: "Inasmuch as these people* [Israel] *draw near with their mouths and honor Me with their lips, but have removed their hearts far from Me, and their fear toward Me is taught by the commandment of men..."*
> (Isaiah 29:13)

Jesus also quoted Isaiah in Matthew 15:7–9, applying the passage to the religious leaders of His day, whom He called "hypocrites." Religious fear is a kind of fear that generates hypocrisy. It is important to remember that the word *hypocrite* is directly derived from the Greek word for an actor, which is *hupokrites*. This is the kind of religious fear that makes people act; their religion consists in a dramatic façade or role-playing. When they enter a church building, they often change their whole demeanor. When they pray, they probably use a special tone of voice. There is nothing genuine or natural; anything they say or do is a performance based on what somebody taught them to do. Jesus said that this artificiality is not what God seeks in His people.

> *Religious fear does not produce obedience that pleases God.*

Religious fear is taught by men, not by God. God does not accept responsibility for it. It is also superficial; it affects outer conduct but leaves the heart unchanged. The Lord says that the people who live in religious fear *"honor Me with their lips, but have removed their hearts far from Me."* Religious fear does not produce the kind of obedience that God desires. It produces a slavish attitude, not the free obedience of sons and daughters, which is what God desires.

Fear of Man

Another kind of fear is the fear of man:

The fear of man brings a snare, but whoever trusts in the LORD shall be safe. (Proverbs 29:25)

The fear of man is the opposite of trust in the Lord. When we are afraid of what people will think or say, we are operating with the fear of man.

We must acknowledge how often the fear of men succeeds in inhibiting us. Times arise when we ought to speak to people about the Lord, but the fear of man prevents us from opening our mouths.

The fear of man makes men more important than God. Those who live with the fear of man are more concerned about what others think about them than what God thinks about them. To these people, God's opinion is less important than the opinion of their fellow men. The fear of man also holds us back from obeying God; it ensnares us when we want to walk in the path of obedience and righteousness.

What the Fear of the Lord *Is*

The fear of the Lord is a special kind of fear; yes, it *is* fear. Sometimes it is experienced physically as a powerful fear. For instance, when Moses was confronted with the glory of the Lord and the voice of the Lord at Mount Sinai, so terrifying was the sight that Moses said, *"I am exceedingly afraid and trembling"* (Hebrews 12:21).

Trembling is not a harmful experience.

Moses probably lived closer than most people to the Lord. But when he was confronted with a revelation of God's majesty and glory, he said, *"I am exceedingly afraid and trembling."* If Moses could tremble, so can we. Trembling is not a harmful experience. In fact, I think most people need a much greater, clearer vision of the awesome majesty and power of God.

Many modern translations of the Bible do not use the word *fear.* I believe that is due—at least in part—to a humanistic attitude that de-emphasizes our need to fear God. But we *do* need to fear God! God is to be feared, and there is nothing in the Bible to suggest that the fear of the Lord is unnecessary or optional.

Think of a towering, craggy mountain, rising up steeply out of the sea. Picture yourself on the pinnacle of this mountain. Looking down one side, you see the waves far below; you can just make out the white foam, and you know that the waves are dashing against the base of the mountain.

You are so high up, however, that you can hardly hear the sound of the crashing waves. Looking down the other side, landward, you see a beautiful array of fields and forests, stretching out to the horizon and illuminated by the shining sun.

You could use a number of adjectives to describe your situation. For instance, it is *beautiful, exhilarating, inspiring,* or *unique.* No sight could parallel it exactly. You enjoy this scene; it uplifts and exhilarates you. But at the same time, somewhere deep inside you, a continual realization reminds you that if you take just one step in the wrong direction, you will be dashed to pieces on the crags and plunged into the sea. You have no intention of taking that step, and yet the very thought of it produces in you a kind of gasp and an involuntary tightening of your diaphragm.

> *The fear of the Lord produces the fruit of submission.*

A word that is related to this hypothetical experience is the word *awe*—as in when we "stand in awe" of someone or something. In a sense, standing in awe means that we do not dare come too close. Another word is *reverence*.

The fear of the Lord is not just one of those words or sensations; rather, it encapsulates all of them. It contains elements of fear, awe, and reverence. An attitude of submission is the fruit produced by the fear of the Lord.

The fear of the Lord is something that we can apprehend only by the Holy Spirit. The fear of the Lord will give us a distinctly unique attitude, regardless of the situation. When we encounter a situation, decision, problem, or need, the fear of the Lord causes us to ask ourselves, *What would God say about this?* That should be our first question—not *What do I think?* or *How can I get what I want out of this?* but *What does God say about this?* The fear of the Lord motivates us to seek to please the Lord always.

Having the fear of the Lord is really the same thing as obeying the first of the Ten Commandments: *"You shall have no other gods before Me"* (Exodus 20:3).

This commandment could also be translated, "You shall have no other gods beside Me." Adhering to this commandment will bring forth the fear of the Lord in our lives. To obey this commandment, we must give God total preeminence.

Nothing else in our lives—no influence, no person, no motivation—should occupy the same level as the Lord God. This expectation is extremely logical, if we think about it. If God is willing to reveal Himself to us—to share Himself with us in some way, to come into our lives—and if almighty God offers us, creatures of dust though we be, the privilege of His fellowship, then why would we even think of offering Him any place but first in our lives?

Genesis 31 includes a remarkable expression that some people may never have noticed. This is part of the scene in which Jacob is confronted by his uncle Laban and they have a strong disagreement. In the end, Laban said, in effect, "If God had not spoken to me, I would have taken vengeance on you." Because God had appeared to Laban and had told him not to harm Jacob, however, he abandoned his violent agenda. Then Jacob said to Laban:

> *Unless the God of my father, the God of Abraham and the Fear of Isaac, had been with me, surely now you would have sent me away empty-handed.*
> (Genesis 31:42)

Take note of the phrase, *"the God of Abraham and the Fear of Isaac."* A little later on in the same chapter, it says Jacob swore and made this oath:

> *"The God of Abraham, the God of Nahor, and the God of their father judge between us." And Jacob swore by the Fear of his father Isaac.*   (verse 53)

Do We Fear the Lord?

Twice, the God of Abraham is called *"the Fear of Isaac."* There must have been something about Isaac's attitude toward God that the Bible does not reveal fully that caused people to talk about God as *"the Fear of Isaac."*

The prophet Isaiah provided a prophetic picture of Jesus. Here is one of the beautiful preliminary descriptions of Jesus. He is called *"the Rod from the stem of Jesse."*

> *There shall come forth a Rod from the stem of Jesse, and a Branch shall grow out of his roots. The Spirit of the LORD shall rest upon Him, The Spirit of wisdom and understanding, The Spirit of counsel and might, The Spirit of knowledge and of the fear of the LORD.*
> (Isaiah 11:1–2)

"Branch" is one of the Old Testament titles for Messiah. And then it says of Him in Revelation:

> *John, to the seven churches which are in Asia: Grace to you and peace from Him who is and who was and who is to come, and from the seven Spirits who are before His throne.* (Revelation 1:4)

Gateway to God's Blessing

In this translation, the word *Spirit* is spelled with a capital *S*. Revelation 4:5 speaks about *"seven lamps of fire"* that are before the throne of God, *"which are the seven Spirits of God."*

Indeed, there is only one Holy Spirit, but He has seven distinctive aspects, otherwise known as manifestations or forms, in which He operates. I believe we can find the seven Spirits, or seven forms, of the Holy Spirit in Isaiah 11:2.

The first one is *"the Lord"*—the Spirit that speaks in the first person as God. In Acts 13:2, Paul wrote that the Holy Spirit said to the church in Antioch, *"Now separate to Me Barnabas and Saul for the work to which I have called them."*

The Holy Spirit spoke to the church in the first person as the Lord. Remember, God the Father is Lord, God the Son is Lord, and God the Spirit is Lord.

Then Isaiah 11:2 says, *"the Spirit of wisdom and understanding."*

Then, *"the Spirit of counsel and might."*

Then, *"the Spirit of knowledge and of the fear of the Lord."*

Seven Aspects of the Holy Spirit

I believe that these are the seven aspects of the Holy Spirit:

1. The Spirit speaking in the first person as God—just as much God as the Father and the Son are God.

2. *"The Spirit of wisdom and understanding."* I am always impressed by the things we need to put together. One may have wisdom, but if he lacks understanding, he will not be able to make the proper use of his wisdom. I was once a professional philosopher, and though I studied wisdom, I did not have much understanding.

3. *"The Spirit of counsel"* (knowing what to do or being able to give direction) combined with (4) *might* (power or strength). It is a terrible thing to have might without counsel. You could end up using your strength the wrong way.

5. *"The Spirit of knowledge and of the fear of the LORD."* Knowledge is wonderful; most people desire it. But by

itself, knowledge puffs up; it makes us inflated. (See 1 Corinthians 8:1.) The Bible nearly always pairs knowledge with the fear of the Lord. We must not seek knowledge unless we have the fear of the Lord; otherwise, knowledge will do us more harm than good.

6. Isaiah 11:3 is a picture of the Messiah, Jesus, whose *"delight is in the fear of the LORD."* Out of the seven aspects given in the previous verses, this aspect is the only one to receive further comment. The one aspect that the Holy Spirit focuses on is (7) *"the fear of the LORD."* If Jesus Himself needed the fear of the Lord, do we not need it as well? The fear of the Lord comes only by the Holy Spirit; without it, we are incomplete and extremely vulnerable to pride and the snares of Satan.

Hebrews 5 provides a remarkable revelation of why God the Father always heard the prayers of Jesus.

> *In the days of His flesh,...He had offered up prayers and supplications, with vehement cries and tears to Him*

who was able to save Him from death, and was heard because of His godly fear, though He was a Son, yet He learned obedience by the things which He suffered. (Hebrews 5:7–8)

God listened to the prayers of Jesus because Jesus always prayed with a godly fear. The passage above refers to a time when He was in agony, waiting in the garden of Gethsemane for His betrayer, Judas, to bring the soldiers who would ultimately crucify Him. In anguish, Jesus prayed to His Father: *"Nevertheless not My will, but Yours, be done"* (Luke 22:42). Such a statement of surrender epitomizes the fear of the Lord. "Lord, let me never put anything of my choice before Yours. Let nothing seem more important to me than Your will." That attitude is the essence of the fear of the Lord.

CHAPTER TEN

The Conditions We Must Meet

There are specific basic requirements that one must fulfill in order to cultivate the fear of the Lord; once this is done, one enters into God's blessings.

The first requirement relates to the theme of decision. Many people wait to call upon God until they are in a desperate situation, but in Proverbs 1, God said that He will not listen to such prayers:

> *Then they will call on me, but I will not answer; They will seek me diligently, but they will not find me. Because*

they hated knowledge And did not choose the fear of the Lord.

(Proverbs 1:28–29)

Again, knowledge and the fear of the Lord are set side by side. Because the people discussed in this passage did not choose the fear of the Lord, God rejected them. The fear of the Lord will not come into our lives unless we choose it; the decision is ours to make.

Let us pray right now: *God, I want to make room in my life for the fear of the Lord. I open up my heart and life to the fear of the Lord. Teach me the fear of the Lord.*

The requirement of making a decision leads to the next requirement, found in Psalm 34. Read what the Holy Spirit speaks to God's children:

Come, you children, listen to me; I will teach you the fear of the Lord. Who is the man who desires life, And loves many days, that he may see good? Keep your tongue from evil, And your lips from speaking deceit.

(Psalm 34:11–13)

We need to be taught the fear of the Lord. After we have chosen it, we have to let the Holy

Spirit teach us the fear of the Lord. There is no instructor besides the Holy Spirit who can teach us the fear of the Lord.

If we allow the Holy Spirit teach us the fear of the Lord, the implication is that we will have life and many days to see good.

That promise is our motivation, and it manifests itself in our speech—the words that come out of our mouth. Does the way in which we speak reflect the fear of the Lord?

> *Do not be wise in your own eyes; Fear the Lord and depart from evil.*
>
> (Proverbs 3:7)

The conditions mentioned here are not trusting in our own wisdom and departing from evil. We must turn our backs on evil and separate ourselves from it. One thing that the Bible makes clear is that evil and the fear of the Lord do not go together.

These are the preliminary conditions that we must fulfill in order to cultivate the fear of the Lord in our lives:

1. We must make the right choice: the fear of the Lord. There are probably some Christians who have never even

been confronted with the necessity of making that choice.

2. We must be taught by the Holy Spirit. He alone can teach us the fear of the Lord. We must enroll as pupils in the school of the Holy Spirit.

3. We must renounce dependence on our own wisdom.

4. We must renounce evil in any form in which we recognize it.

CHAPTER ELEVEN

Benefits and Blessings

The fear of the Lord is the only source of wisdom. Let us now consider what the fear of the Lord will do for us. Here is an easy text to remember: Job 28:28.

> *And to man He [God] said, "Behold, the fear of the Lord, that is wisdom, and to depart from evil is understanding."*

If we read the verses preceding verse 28 in Job chapter 28, we see that God's wisdom is expressed throughout the entire universe. Everything in the universe expresses some aspect of God's wisdom. The total wisdom of God is staggering; our finite minds cannot comprehend it. But God says, in essence, "If you want access to My wisdom—if you want Me to begin to release My wisdom into your life—then there is one channel through which it can come to you: the fear of the Lord." The only way that man can attain true wisdom is through the fear of the Lord—and through living a life of righteousness. *"To depart from evil is understanding."* It is important that we recognize the moral foundation of wisdom.

> *The fear of the LORD is the beginning of wisdom; a good understanding have all those who do His commandments.*
> (Psalm 111:10)

The word translated as *beginning* can also mean "the principal part"—it is the basis and foundation of all wisdom. Again, understanding is linked with obedience to the commandments of God. It has a moral aspect.

Out of wisdom proceeds understanding. In its original Hebrews form, the word *understanding* signifies insight into the true nature and essence of persons and situations—it means much more than mere cleverness. Even a clever person can be fooled, sometimes by other people. But a person with understanding sees into the very nature of the person he is dealing with and the very essence of the situation that he has to handle.

> *The fear of the LORD is the beginning of knowledge, But fools despise wisdom and instruction.* (Proverbs 1:7)

Again, *beginning* means "the principal part of"—the fear of the Lord is the principal part of knowledge.

Looking at these last three Scripture passages, we see that the fear of the Lord develops wisdom, first of all; then understanding, or insight; and finally, knowledge. But the writer of Proverbs went on to say, *"but fools despise wisdom and instruction."* To despise instruction—to be proud, self-sufficient, arrogant, unwilling to accept correction—is folly. And folly automatically excludes true wisdom; it is the exact opposite of the fear of the Lord.

> *The fear of the LORD is the beginning of wisdom, And the knowledge of the Holy One is understanding.* (Proverbs 9:10)

Out of the fear of the Lord comes a wisdom that enables us to relate to God's holiness. And as we relate to God's holiness, we move and live in the cleansing, sanctifying fear of the

Lord that causes us to depart from evil and to keep the Lord's commandments.

We need to distinguish between wisdom and intellectual education. It is possible to be highly educated and to remain a fool. Much of the trouble in the world today is caused by educated fools.

Wisdom, as spoken of in Scripture, differs significantly from intellect, education, or scholarly learning. In Psalm 51, David came to the very heart of this matter. Speaking to the Lord from a broken, penitent heart, he wrote:

Behold, You desire truth in the inward parts, And in the hidden part You will make me to know wisdom.

(Psalm 51:6)

God desires truth in the inward parts—truth that comes from the fear of the Lord. When we have truth in the inward part—when we are sincere, upright, and open with God—He promises to *"make* [us] *to know wisdom."*

Wisdom is not the same as intellect. Rather than being in the mind, wisdom is in the hidden part of man—his spirit, his innermost depths. The hidden part of man is where

God wants us to cultivate the fear of the Lord so that we may receive His wisdom.

The only channel through which to receive the wisdom of God is the fear of the Lord. There is no other way that God's wisdom can come into our lives but through the fear of the Lord. His wisdom will not primarily affect our intellectual capacities, although it will illuminate our intellect.

When we have God's wisdom, we receive His counsel.

It will not be a substitute for education; it will not do for us what education will do. God's wisdom is entirely unique. It comes into our spirits and opens our eyes so that we can begin to see God's purposes—to see our life and the things around us in the light of divine purpose and divine counsel.

In Scripture, counsel is closely related to wisdom. When we have God's wisdom, we receive His counsel. With God's counsel, we know how to act in different situations; we know how to relate to different people and how to help them.

Ecclesiastes 10:10 says, *"Wisdom is profitable to direct"* (KJV). Wisdom shows us the way to go; it steers us past life's pitfalls, snares, and disguised dangers.

Wisdom is found in the hidden part—in the innermost chamber of man's spirit. There is only one avenue to the hidden part in man, but we cannot achieve it by intellectual education.

Instead, we must open up to God, who will impart His wisdom into our hidden parts via one channel: the fear of the Lord. We must ask God to open up that channel to us.

In the Psalms

Serve the LORD with fear, And rejoice with trembling. (Psalm 2:11)

We are not instructed simply to serve the Lord, but to *"serve the Lord with fear."* Our natural minds struggle, however, to comprehend the second part of that verse. We think, *If there is fear, I cannot rejoice; if I am rejoicing, there is no room for fear.* Our natural inclination is to think that fear and rejoicing are mutually exclusive. This is not the case, however.

We must learn that we have a right to rejoice. In the spiritual realm, it is actually the fear of the Lord that releases rejoicing. Without the fear of the Lord, our rejoicing is shallow, unsubstantial, and impermanent. The combination of fear and rejoicing brings success in the Christian life. Our spiritual safety is secured by a balance between the fear of the Lord and rejoicing in the Lord.

We receive the wisdom of God only when we fear the Lord.

I do not believe in making fun of people who respond differently to God. I may respond one way; others may respond differently. But if a response to God is genuine, I am determined to respect it, regardless of its manifestation.

I was raised in the Anglican Church. When I discovered that many other denominations and sects besides Anglicanism existed, I used to make fun of them.

For example, I would mock people who were serious and quiet. I thought they were lacking in liberty. But I stopped making fun when I realized that there are different ways that human beings respond to God.

135

Regardless of our particular denomination or church, regardless of our response to God, we must put together rejoicing and trembling.

> *Who is the man that fears the LORD? Him shall He teach in the way He* [the Lord] *chooses. The secret of the LORD is with those who fear Him, And He will show them His covenant.*
>
> (Psalm 25:12, 14)

God will teach the one who hears Him; He will teach him in the way that He chooses. I have told people time and again that we can enroll in any Bible college or seminary, but that is no guarantee that the Lord will teach us, because the Lord chooses His students on the basis of their character. And the primary character requirement is fear of the Lord.

Verse 14 makes what I consider to be one of the most amazing statements in Scripture: *"The secret of the LORD is with those who fear Him."* The *New International Version* translates this verse, *"The LORD confides in those who fear Him"*—He shares His secrets. What a privilege to share in the secrets of the Lord!

> *The fear of the LORD is clean, enduring forever....* (Psalm 19:9)

"The fear of the Lord is clean." What a beautiful statement. There is a cleansing power in the fear of the Lord that keeps us from the defilement of sin and the contamination of this world.

The world in which we live is extremely contaminated. We worry about pollution, which is contamination in the physical realm, but much worse is pollution in the spiritual realm. So much of what we hear, read, or watch on television—much of what surrounds us in our work-

We must both rejoice and tremble.

places and elsewhere—is impure. Impurities break down our moral fiber. We need something to protect us—something to preserve us from the world's contamination.

The psalmist pointed us to God's provision: *"The fear of the Lord is clean, enduring forever."* The fear of the Lord has no end; it is infinite. It is a permanent requirement of God and a permanent provision of God.

Come, you children, listen to me; I will teach you the fear of the Lord. Who is the man who desires life, and loves many days, that he may see good? Keep your tongue from evil, and your lips from speaking deceit. Depart from evil and do good; seek peace and pursue it.

(Psalm 34:11–14)

Here the Holy Spirit brings out certain extremely important features of the fear of the Lord. First, the fear of the Lord must be taught. The Holy Spirit says, *"I will teach you the fear of the LORD"* (verse 11). If we are not willing to be taught—if we are not willing to receive counsel and correction—then we cannot receive the fear of the Lord.

The fear of the Lord does not compromise with evil.

Second, the psalmist said that the first area of our lives in which the fear of the Lord will be manifested is our tongues—the words that we speak. *"Keep your tongue from evil"* (verse 13). A person who does not control his tongue is not walking in the fear of the Lord. The fear of the Lord manifests itself in words that are chosen carefully—words spoken without exaggeration or foolishness.

Benefits and Blessings

The third feature emphasized in this passage is that the fear of the Lord leaves no room for compromise with evil. We are told, *"Depart from evil and do good"* (verse 14). The fear of the Lord offers us life—many days that we may see good.

This fact is emphasized continually in the books of Psalms and Proverbs. The fear of the Lord brings us life—a good, long life of many days. Psalm 128 provides a beautiful picture of the man who fears the Lord and receives many blessings as a result:

> *Blessed are all who fear the Lord, who walk in his ways. You will eat the fruit of your labor; blessings and prosperity will be yours. Your wife will be like a fruitful vine within your house; your sons will be like olive shoots around your table. Thus is the man blessed who fears the Lord.* (Psalm 128:1–4 NIV)

What all-inclusive blessings: blessings for the man, for his work, for his home, for his wife, and for his children. *"Blessings and prosperity will be yours"*—all these are promised to the man who fears the Lord and walks in His ways.

In Proverbs

We have seen that the fear of the Lord is the only source of true wisdom. In the first chapter of Proverbs, wisdom is personified as a woman who makes a dramatic appeal to the entire human race:

> *Wisdom calls aloud outside; she raises her voice in the open squares. She cries out in the chief concourses, at the openings of the gates in the city she speaks her words: "How long, you simple ones, will you love simplicity? For scorners delight in their scorning, and fools hate knowledge. Turn at my rebuke; surely I will pour out my spirit on you; I will make my words known to you."*
>
> (Proverbs 1:20–23)

The opening verse mentions places of meeting where people gather—the places where the greatest number of people can be addressed. Thus, wisdom makes her appeal to the entire human race.

Behind the personification of wisdom is the Lord Himself. He says, in essence, "If, when I reprove you, you repent and turn back to Me, I will pour out My Spirit on you; I will make

My words known to you." The Holy Spirit alone can make known to us the words of God. And then, God speaks to the stubborn and the rebellious:

> *Because I have called and you refused, I have stretched out my hand and no one regarded, because you disdained all my counsel, and would have none of my rebuke, I also will laugh at your calamity; I will mock when your terror comes, when your terror comes like a storm, and your destruction comes like a whirlwind, when distress and anguish come upon you. Then they will call on me, but I will not answer; they will seek me diligently, but they will not find me. Because they hated knowledge and* **did not choose the fear of the Lord,** *they would have none of my counsel and despised my every rebuke.*
> (Proverbs 1:24–30, emphasis added)

Again, the fear of the Lord will come into our lives when we make a choice. We have to choose the fear of the Lord, which is the opposite of disdaining His counsel and rebuke. We have to exercise our will. We have to decide to invite God to impart to us the fear of the Lord. This does not just happen. We must cooperate with our will in this process.

If we do not make an intentional choice, then the fear of the Lord will not be ours; we will find ourselves categorized with those who would not receive God's counsel and who despised His rebuke. The consequences of rejecting wisdom and the fear of the Lord are distress and anguish.

Rejecting God's rebuke invites anguish.

Here is a clear watershed: we either invite God to teach us the fear of the Lord or turn away, despising His counsel and rejecting His rebuke. If we have the fear of the Lord, all the blessings we have discussed shall be ours. But if we reject God's counsel and rebuke, and if we do not open our hearts to receive the fear of the Lord, then we must expect distress and anguish.

Wisdom continues to make her fervent appeal to humanity. Humanity has not changed. People's hearts and ways have not changed from how they were when the Bible was written.

And God has not changed. He still speaks to people today, saying, in essence, "Stop! Think about your ways! Listen for a moment, for I have sound advice for you. I have counsel. I am willing to teach you something that will bring My blessings in their fullness into your lives."

> *The fear of the Lord is to hate evil; pride and arrogance and the evil way and the perverse mouth I hate.* (Proverbs 8:13)

Again, wisdom is speaking—she tells us that the nature of the fear of the Lord is to hate evil. We see again and again, throughout the Scriptures, that the fear of the Lord permits no compromise with evil. If we have the fear of the Lord, we will in no way tolerate evil or compromise with it. Instead, we will hate evil, rejecting it and allowing it no room anywhere in our lives.

Another fact that is repeated in the verse above is that the fear of the Lord will be manifested in the way we use our mouths and our tongues. Wisdom says, *"The fear of the Lord is to hate evil; the perverse mouth I hate."* The fear of the Lord will direct how we use our tongues.

Gateway to God's Blessing

> *In mercy and truth atonement is provided for iniquity; and by the fear of the LORD one departs from evil.*
>
> (Proverbs 16:6)

The same truth appears again: the fear of the Lord leaves no room for compromise with evil. Those who have the fear of the Lord will hate evil; that is their inner attitude. We must depart from evil. Departing from evil is an outward action that leaves no room for compromise.

> *The fear of the LORD prolongs days, but the years of the wicked will be shortened.* (Proverbs 10:27)

> *In the fear of the LORD there is strong confidence, and His children will have a place of refuge.* (Proverbs 14:26)

When we cultivate the fear of the Lord, we will have strong confidence. We will not be easily frightened or upset. God promises a place of refuge for our children. When we choose life and blessing, this decision will affect our descendants.

The one who has the fear of the Lord can expect a place of refuge for his children.

Believe me, in this world, it is important to have a place of refuge.

> *The fear of the Lord is a fountain of life, to turn one away from the snares of death.* (Proverbs 14:27)

> *The fear of the Lord leads to life, and he who has it will abide in satisfaction; he will not be visited with evil.*
> (Proverbs 19:23)

This is one of the most amazing verses in the Bible. I know of no verse that promises more than this verse. If we have the fear of the Lord, we will be permanently satisfied. Conversely, if we are frustrated and dissatisfied, our lives lack the fear of the Lord.

In addition to bringing lasting satisfaction, the fear of the Lord keeps us from being visited with evil. We could spend hours just contemplating these three promises about the fear of the Lord: it leads to life, we will abide in satisfaction, and we will not be visited with evil.

> *By humility and the fear of the Lord are riches and honor and life.*
> (Proverbs 22:4)

We must combine humility with the fear of the Lord. It is impossible, in fact, to combine the opposite of humility—pride—with the fear of the Lord. We have already discussed this truth. When we practice humility and have the fear of the Lord, we are promised riches, honor, and life.

> *Do not let your heart envy sinners, but be zealous for the fear of the LORD all the day; for surely there is a hereafter, and your hope will not be cut off.*
> (Proverbs 23:17–18)

We must be zealous in our fear of the Lord all day long. The fear of the Lord should permeate our lives and direct our lifestyles. I believe that a person who lives and walks in the fear of the Lord will have a distinctively different—and extremely attractive—lifestyle.

The fear of the Lord is not just something that we practice sporadically, at certain moments—like when we go to church. Some people become extremely reverent in church, but when they walk out of church, they lay aside their reverence and resume their normal behavior—behavior that does not reflect the fear of the Lord.

But the Scripture tells us to continue in the fear of the Lord all day long and not to envy sinners. We are not to be enticed by the apparent pleasures of sin, which are temporary and frustrating.

The final promise of this passage from Proverbs is beautiful: *"For surely there is a hereafter, and your hope will not be cut off"* (verse 18). There is a hereafter for all people, regardless of whether they acknowledge this truth. For those who continue in the fear of the Lord, the promise of a hereafter is filled

The fear of the Lord should permeate our lives.

with hope. The ultimate benefit of the fear of the Lord goes beyond time and into eternity. Its benefits are not limited to life on earth; rather, they extend eternally. The fear of the Lord gives us a hope that extends beyond the grave—a hope that will never be disappointed. That is what God's Word promises.

Life and the fear of the Lord go together. If we desire full, abundant, satisfying lives, we must cultivate the fear of the Lord. Those who have not made this choice should do so now.

Again and again—especially in the books of Psalms and Proverbs—the fear of the Lord is linked with long life and good days. The fear of the Lord prolongs our days.

Those who do not fear the Lord, on the other hand, are wicked; their days will be shortened. (See Proverbs 10:27.)

In Psalm 34, the Holy Spirit speaks through the psalmist to say, in essence, "Do you want to lead a long and a good life and see many days? Cultivate the fear of the Lord."

Here, the message is the same: the fear of the Lord makes provision not just for length of life, but for quality of life. It is not just a long life; it is good days, that you may see good.

Here are some of the many benefits and blessings, listed in the books of Psalms and Proverbs, that are promised to us if we practice the fear of the Lord. By no means do I suggest that this list is comprehensive, however.

Benefits and Blessings

First, **continual spiritual cleansing**. *"The fear of the LORD is clean, enduring forever"* (Psalm 19:9).

Second, **life** and **many good days**. There are at least half a dozen different passages where life in its fullness—in both quantity and quality—is associated with the fear of the Lord.

Third, **a blessed and happy family**. This is the promise in Psalm 128. It covers the man, his wife, his children, and his job.

Fourth, **freedom from all evil fears**. *"In the fear of the LORD there is strong confidence"* (Proverbs 14:26).

Fifth, **a place of security**—a shelter (Proverbs 14:26).

Sixth, **deliverance from satanic snares** that would entrap us and bring about death, both physical and spiritual.

Seventh, **abiding satisfaction**. *"He who has it* [the fear of the Lord] *will abide in satisfaction"* (Proverbs 19:23). What a staggering promise! So few people seem to be truly and permanently satisfied—yet true, permanent satisfaction is promised through the fear of the Lord.

Eighth, **preservation from the visitation of evil**. *"He will not be visited with evil"* (Proverbs 19:23).

Ninth, **riches and honor**.

And tenth, **a hope that extends beyond the grave**.

Those are just some of the many blessings and benefits that are promised to those who cultivate the fear of the Lord.

CHAPTER TWELVE

The Key to a Perfect Heart

W e will now examine a scriptural sketch of the kind of person who is qualified to enter into God's blessings. The first verse we will look at is found in 2 Chronicles, and I believe it to be one of the most remarkable statements in Scripture.

> *For the eyes of the LORD run to and fro throughout the whole earth, to show himself strong in the behalf of them whose heart is perfect toward him.*
> (2 Chronicles 16:9 KJV)

The eyes of the Lord—which is a phrase that refers to the Holy Spirit—are looking for a certain kind of person, wherever he might exist on earth. They are looking for someone whose heart is perfect toward God, so that God can show Himself strong on that person's behalf.

Here is a more modern rendering of this verse:

> *For the eyes of the LORD range throughout the earth to strengthen those whose hearts are fully committed to him.*
>
> (2 Chronicles 16:9 NIV)

To have a "perfect heart" is to turn the entirety of one's heart toward the Lord; no part of it is turned away from the Lord. The entire heart of such a person is focused on the Lord. His entire attitude is encapsulated in the questions, "How can I please the Lord? What does the Lord require of me? How does the Lord view this situation? How does the Lord view this choice that I am going to make?" There is no area of such a person's

> *We must "burn our bridges" and step out in faith.*

heart that seeks to turn away from the Lord or tries to hide anything from Him.

The *New International Version* translation is equally beautiful: *"whose hearts are fully committed to him."* Full commitment is essential for the fear of the Lord. Those who fear the Lord are totally committed to God's way—to pleasing Him and doing His will.

In a certain sense, those who commit themselves to the Lord must "burn their bridges." There is no way back; they have taken a decisive step.

In the Bible, most of the people who were called into the Lord's service had to burn their bridges in some respect. They had to make an irrevocable commitment. There was no going back; it was all or nothing.

This requirement holds true today in the lives of those who would serve the Lord. I know it was true in my own life. I can look back on more than one situation where, in order to do the will of God, I had to make a commitment that was irrevocable. There was no way to undo it; there was no turning back.

If God confronts us with such a commitment, we should not be afraid to make it. When we burn our bridges and step out in faith, God will open up things for us that we never would have discovered otherwise. We must make a commitment to Him.

Let us meditate on those two translations: *"whose heart is perfect toward [the L*ORD*]"* and *"whose hearts are fully committed to him."* We must ask ourselves whether our hearts are perfect toward the Lord, and whether they are fully committed to Him.

A person whose heart is committed to God views everything from His perspective.

A person whose heart is perfect toward the Lord and is committed to Him views every issue from God's perspective. He asks, "How does *God* see this?" not, "How will this work out for *me*? How will this affect *me*? Where are *my* interests?"

The attitude that seeks God's perspective eclipses all other motives and pressures, overruling them. We know from experience that there are many pressures in our lives—pressures from society, culture, the media, the marketplace—that try to cause us to do things. But these things may or may not be what God wants us to do.

A brief example would be the fear of public opinion. Many people allow their lives to be molded by the fear of what other people might think or say. This fear is improper motivation.

Another improper motivation is self-interest—going after promotion, fame, or wealth.

Yet another improper kind of motivation popular today is sensual indulgence—the pursuit of pleasure. We see countless people who are motivated by one or more of these pressures.

People who are ruled by these motives are easily swayed. They are unstable and undependable; we cannot rely on them. They have never cultivated the fear of the Lord.

In Jeremiah 17, we see a picture of two kinds of people: one is blessed; the other is cursed.

This is what the LORD says: "Cursed is the one who trusts in man, who depends on flesh for his strength and whose heart turns away from the LORD. He will

be like a bush in the wastelands; he
will not see prosperity when it comes.
He will dwell in the parched places of
the desert, in a salt land where no one
lives." (Jeremiah 17:5–6 NIV)

This passage is a picture of the man who is cursed—his problem is that his heart has turned away from the Lord. His heart is not perfect toward the Lord, and he is relying on himself—his own cleverness, effort, and abilities. He is making his own plans and choices. Now, let us look at the man who is blessed:

But blessed is the man who trusts in the
Lord, whose confidence is in him. He
will be like a tree planted by the water
that sends out its roots by the stream.
It does not fear when heat comes; its
leaves are always green. It has no wor-
ries in a year of drought and never fails
to bear fruit. (verses 7–8 NIV)

What a beautiful picture. When our confidence is in the Lord, we will not fear when heat comes. The fear of the Lord eliminates those negative fears.

Like healthy trees, we are fresh and green. We are never frazzled or withered; we are never parched or thirsty. We have no worries in a year of drought. Does not everyone want to be like that? To have no worries, even in a year of drought, when everybody else is thirsty and desperate?

Our roots go to the source of life: God Himself.

We never fail to bear fruit. A fruited tree is a symbolic picture of the one who walks and lives in the fear of the Lord—one whose heart is perfect toward God, who is fully committed to God.

We are left with some decisive questions to answer. How deep do our roots go? What is the source of our lives? With the fear of the Lord, our roots go down to the source of life: God Himself.

Pictures of the Fear of the Lord

These pictures that represent the fear of the Lord are found in the experience of God's people. In the New Testament, we see a summation of the growth of the Christian church early in its history. This is a description of the early churches in Judea, Galilee, and Samaria. They had passed through a time of persecution stirred up primarily by Saul of Tarsus, who was later converted and became the apostle Paul. Out of the time of persecution, the churches had entered into a time of rest and blessing.

> *Then the churches throughout all Judea, Galilee, and Samaria had peace and were edified. And walking in the fear of the Lord and in the comfort of the Holy Spirit, they were multiplied.* (Acts 9:31)

Two characteristics are coupled together: *"the fear of the Lord"* and *"the comfort* [or encouragement] *of the Holy Spirit."* It is so easy to have a polarized viewpoint—to think that it is all comfort or all fear; it is all rejoicing or all trembling. Again, only the Holy Spirit can give us the balance, and it is the balance that brings the blessing.

Many of us would say, "What I really need is comfort, encouragement, or truth." But if we receive comfort and encouragement without the fear of the Lord in our lives, they will not last or meet our deepest needs.

Comfort and encouragement without the fear of the Lord are liable to make us careless, proud, or puffed up. By themselves, they will not produce the result that is needed—the result that God intends. The comfort of the Holy Spirit must be balanced by the fear of the Lord—the reverent awe of the Lord, which is also inspired by the Holy Spirit. We must not separate these two things. I want to suggest further that we should not reverse the order. In other words,

A balance of fear and comfort brings a blessing.

we should not put comfort before fear, even though the tendency to do so is common for most people. The divinely inspired Word of God puts the fear of the Lord first, followed by the comfort of the Lord. I believe that we each find safety in this order.

Let us consider the results when this order was followed in the early churches: they had peace, were edified, and were multiplied. These three results in the Christian church also come to the lives of Christians who achieve a balance between the fear of the Lord and the comfort of the Holy Spirit.

First of all, the churches had peace. Other kinds of fear do not impart peace; it is a unique result of the fear of the Lord.

Second, they were edified or built up—they grew stronger.

And third, they were multiplied—their numbers grew. If we achieve multiplication but do not begin with the fear of the Lord, the results are likely to be superficial and temporary. I have seen churches grow like mushrooms—and wither like fungus. They withered because they were not rooted in the fear of the Lord.

The apostle Paul had been talking about being continually filled—not filled just once, but filled continually—with the Holy Spirit, speaking to ourselves or to one another with psalms, hymns, and spiritual songs (verses 18–20). Then, in Ephesians 5:21, he identified the type of lifestyle this leads to: a lifestyle characterized by *"submitting to one another in the fear of God."*

Submission indicates that one is filled with the Holy Spirit.

Submissiveness is an indication that someone is filled with the Holy Spirit. The primary relationship of submission within the body of

The Key to a Perfect Heart

Christ is not to the leaders but to one another. Other verses speak about submitting to the leaders, but the primary submission within the body of Christ is each of us submitting to one another. Leaders who have not learned to submit should not be leading. Peter warned us not to be lords over God's flock but to be an example. (See 1 Peter 5:1–5.) In that context, he said to put on the apron of slavery and serve one another.

Paul went on: *"Wives, submit to your own husbands, as to the Lord"* (Ephesians 5:22). Of course, this is directed toward wives—but in the previous verses, Paul was talking about mutual submission.

I once counseled a man who was a successful Baptist pastor. He had built a large congregation and had written several books. Outwardly, he was extremely successful, but he shared with me that his home life and his marriage were far from successful. Such is the case in many such ministries, unfortunately. But he shared a story that blessed me.

He and his wife were in their bedroom, kneeling down on opposite sides of the bed and trying to pray. They had just had an argument. Like the typical pastor husband, he had told his wife, "But the Bible says you have to submit to me!" And his wife replied, "Well, you do not have such a good record. I do not know why I should."

They were headed for a real debate. Then, he told me, "Something like a cold wind blew through the bedroom, and we realized it was the fear of God." We cannot hope to have successful relationships without first having the fear of God. At the same time, they both realized that it was not a question of how the husband treated his wife or how the wife responded to her husband. The question was, "Do we fear God?"

Successful relationships depend on the fear of the Lord.

That question should be the driving motivation behind every relationship. It is not an issue of human personalities; rather, it is an issue of God Himself and His requirement. He requires that we be submissive to one another: that husbands submit to Him, that wives submit to their husbands, that children submit to their parents. If we want to receive the blessing of the Lord, we have to meet His conditions.

The Key to a Perfect Heart

Let us look at one final great, unchanging reason why all of us need to cultivate the fear of the Lord in our lives.

> *But as He who called you is holy, you also be holy in all your conduct, because it is written, "Be holy, for I am holy." And if you call on the Father, who without partiality judges according to each one's work, conduct yourselves throughout the time of your stay here* **in fear**; *knowing that you were not redeemed with corruptible things, like silver or gold, from your aimless conduct received by tradition from your fathers, but with the precious blood of Christ, as of a lamb without blemish and without spot.*
>
> (1 Peter 1:15–19, emphasis added)

Those words are not addressed to sinners. They are addressed to God's people, who believe in Him and have been redeemed. It is to them that Peter said, *"Conduct yourselves throughout the time of your stay here in fear"* (1 Peter 1:17). And he gave two reasons that we need to have this attitude of reverent fear.

First of all, he said, we will all be required to give an account of ourselves to God, our

Father. There is a judgment awaiting all of us. It is not a judgment of condemnation, but it is a judgment that will evaluate our lives—our services and our faithfulness. As Paul wrote in 2 Corinthians 5:10, *"For we must all appear before the judgment seat of Christ, that each one may receive the things done in the body, according to what he has done, whether good or bad."* I believe that we must each keep this realization continually before us.

Second, we need to have reverent fear because of the great price that God was willing to pay for our redemption. We were *"not redeemed with corruptible things, like silver or gold...but with the precious blood of Christ, as of a lamb without blemish and without spot"* (1 Peter 1:18–19). The most precious thing in the universe was paid for our redemption. The gravity of that truth should cause us to live in the reverent fear of the Lord, lest we do anything that would displease or dishonor the One who paid such a tremendous price for us.

CHAPTER THIRTEEN

Our Response

There are four important steps that I believe will lead us to this desirable end—having the fear of the Lord in our lives.

The first step is found in a passage in Proverbs 1, which we have discussed more than once already. Wisdom is personified, and she makes an appeal to men. The verse indicates that many people turn down this appeal and reject wisdom's offer:

Then they will call on me, but I will not answer; they will seek me diligently, but they will not find me. Because they hated knowledge and did not choose the fear of the LORD, they would have none of my counsel and despised my every rebuke. (Proverbs 1:28–30)

In order to enter into the fear of the Lord, the first thing we must do is make a definite, personal choice. We must say, "Lord, I choose to take the course that will lead me into the fear of the Lord, whatever it means. I am willing; I make this choice; I make this decision."

Anyone who has yet to make this decision can make it right now by saying in their heart to the Lord, "Lord, I make this choice; I choose the fear of the Lord. Lead me into it."

The second requirement, which is also stated in this passage from Proverbs, is to accept counsel and rebuke. Wisdom says of these people who did not find the fear of the Lord, *"They would have none of my counsel and despised my every rebuke"* (verse 30)— they were uncorrectable and unteachable.

Step two is turning ourselves to the source that teaches us the fear of the Lord: the Holy Spirit. We have already looked at the passage in Psalm 34:11 where the Holy Spirit, on behalf of God, is speaking to God's children and says, *"Come, you children, listen to me; I will teach you the fear of the LORD."*

Our Response

In order to enter into the fear of the Lord, we have to be willing to be taught by the Holy Spirit. And in order to be taught, we have to listen. It is impolite to turn away and ignore someone who is seeking to speak to us—we will not receive whatever he or she has to say. I am afraid that many times, God's children treat the Holy Spirit impolitely. He is seeking to speak to us, but we have other ideas and personal priorities, so we do not hear; we do not learn.

We must choose the fear of the Lord.

If we have made the decision to seek the fear of the Lord, we must turn ourselves over to the Holy Spirit and say, "Holy Spirit, be our teacher; we really want to listen. Help us to hear, and as we hear, help us to learn." We must cultivate a sensitivity to the Holy Spirit. Without that, we will not find the fear of the Lord. He is the guide, the teacher. He is the one who speaks to the children of God and says, *"Come, you children, listen to me; I will teach you the fear of the Lord."*

The third step in cultivating the fear of the Lord turns us to human ministers. There are two passages in the book of Hebrews that

speak about our attitude toward the ministers of God. God has appointed people of His choosing in the body of Christ to rule and to fulfill other functions. Some people have the attitude that says, "I will listen to God if He has something to say to me, but I do not have to learn from men."

If someone says, "I will listen to the Holy Spirit, but I am not going to accept teaching from men," he or she is tying the hands of the Holy Spirit.

We have no right to do that. The Holy Spirit may want to teach us through a pastor, an evangelist, or a Bible teacher on a radio program. We must be willing to accept the Holy Spirit's teaching by whatever channel God uses to make it available to us.

> *Remember those who rule over you, who have spoken the word of God to you, whose faith follow, considering the outcome of their conduct....Obey those who rule over you, and be submissive, for they watch out for your souls, as those who must give account. Let them do so with joy and not with grief, for that would be unprofitable for you."*
>
> (Hebrews 13:7, 17)

Our Response

God has placed within the body of Christ people who rule, who set an example of faith. These individuals speak the Word of God and watch over our souls. If we are going to learn the fear of the Lord, it is vitally important that we submit to the people whom God places in our lives.

> *He Himself gave some to be apostles, some prophets, some evangelists, and some pastors and teachers, for the equipping of the saints for the work of ministry, for the edifying of the body of Christ.* (Ephesians 4:11–12)

God has placed specific people in the church to help us become the kind of people He wants us to be.

Step four is to seek to be taught by the Word of God itself. This step is taken from Proverbs 2, where God is speaking to His child. There are four verses leading up to the climax, and each verse contains a pair:

> *My son, if you receive my words, and treasure my commands within you, so that you incline your ear to wisdom, and apply your heart to understanding; yes, if you cry out for discernment, and lift up your voice for understanding, if*

you seek her as silver, and search for her as for hidden treasures; then you will understand the fear of the LORD, and find the knowledge of God.

(Proverbs 2:1–5)

The first pair comprises the acts of receiving God's Word and treasuring His commands within us. Then, the word *incline* means to bow down. That means to be teachable or humble.

So the next thing we have to do is bow down our ears and apply our hearts to wisdom and understanding. The third pair says to *"cry out"* and *"lift up your voice."* In one word, these two phrases refer to *prayer*—fervent, impassioned prayer. We cry out, "God, we must have this. We will not cease praying until You grant it to us."

Verse four talks about seeking—continual seeking. If someone heard there was a large treasure buried in the local park, and that he could have the entire treasure if he could find it, would he not go out there and immediately start to dig? Would he worry about the blisters on his hands? Few things come into the Christian life without hard work. It starts with the treasure, but the treasure is gained by our own zeal and diligence.

Our Response

Again, there are four conditions we must meet:

1. We must receive God's Word and treasure His commands.

2. We must incline our ears to wisdom and apply our hearts to understanding.

3. We must cry out for discernment and lift up our voices for understanding.

4. We must seek wisdom as silver, and search for her as hidden treasure.

The conclusion of this passage from Proverbs bears repeating: *"Then you will understand the fear of the LORD, and find the knowledge of God"* (verse 5).

Notice that the knowledge and the fear of the Lord go together. They are seldom separated. The climax is to understand the fear of the Lord and find the knowledge of God.

Nothing could ever be greater than to find the knowledge of God and to come to know Him—the eternal, almighty, omnipotent, omniscient Creator. But can we ever come to know Him? Yes, we can, if we will meet the conditions—but never without the fear of the

Lord. First, we must understand the fear of the Lord, and only then can we find the knowledge of God.

Have we perhaps now gained a deep desire for the fear of the Lord? Are we willing to meet the conditions? How will we respond to God's offer, which is also a challenge? I do not believe that God has ever promised anything that we cannot have. So we can understand the fear of the Lord and find the knowledge of God—which throws open wide the gateway to God's innumerable blessings.

About the Author

Derek Prince

Derek Prince (1915–2003) was born in Bangalore, India, into a British military family. He was educated as a scholar of classical languages (Greek, Latin, Hebrew, and Aramaic) at Eton College and Cambridge University in England, and later at Hebrew University, Israel. As a student, he was a philosopher and self-proclaimed atheist. He held a fellowship in ancient and modern philosophy at King's College, Cambridge.

While in the British Medical Corps during World War II, Prince began to study the Bible as a philosophical work. Converted through a powerful encounter with Jesus Christ, he was baptized in the Holy Spirit a few days later.

GATEWAY TO GOD'S BLESSING

This life-changing experience altered the whole course of his life, which he thereafter devoted to studying and teaching the Bible as the Word of God.

Discharged from the army in Jerusalem in 1945, he married Lydia Christensen, founder of a children's home there. Upon their marriage, he immediately became father to Lydia's eight adopted daughters—six Jewish, one Palestinian Arab, and one English. Together, the family saw the rebirth of the state of Israel in 1948. In the late 1950s, the Princes adopted another daughter while Derek was serving as principal of a college in Kenya.

In 1963, the Princes immigrated to the United States and pastored a church in Seattle, Washington. Stirred by the tragedy of President John F. Kennedy's assassination, Prince began to teach Americans how to intercede for their nation. In 1973, he became one of the founders of Intercessors for America. His book *Shaping History through Prayer and Fasting* has awakened Christians around the world to their responsibility to pray for their governments. Many consider underground translations of the book as having been instrumental in the fall of communist regimes in the former USSR, East Germany, and Czechoslovakia.

About the Author

Lydia Prince died in 1975, and Derek married Ruth Baker, a single mother of three adopted children, in 1978. He met his second wife, like the first, while she was serving the Lord in Jerusalem. Ruth died in December 1998 in Jerusalem, where they had lived since 1981.

Until a few years before his own death in 2003 at the age of eighty-eight, Prince persisted in the ministry God had called him to as he traveled the world, imparting God's revealed truth, praying for the sick and afflicted, and sharing his prophetic insights into world events in the light of Scripture. He wrote more than fifty books, which have been translated into more than sixty languages and distributed worldwide. He pioneered teaching on such ground-breaking themes as generational curses, the biblical significance of Israel, and demonology.

Derek Prince Ministries, with its international headquarters in Charlotte, North Carolina, continues to distribute his teachings and to train missionaries, church leaders, and congregations through worldwide branch offices. Prince's radio program, *Keys to Successful Living* (now known as *Derek Prince Legacy Radio*), began in 1979 and has been translated into more than a dozen languages. Estimates are that Derek Prince's clear, non-denominational, nonsectarian teaching of the Bible has reached more than half the globe.

Internationally recognized as a Bible scholar and spiritual patriarch, Derek Prince established a teaching ministry that spanned six continents and more than sixty years. In 2002, he said, "It is my desire—and I believe the Lord's desire—that this ministry continue the work, which God began through me over sixty years ago, until Jesus returns."